The Teacher
as a Person

The Teacher as a Person

•

Edited by

Luiz F.S. Natalicio
University of Texas at El Paso

Carl F. Hereford
The University of Texas at Austin

Second Edition

WM. C. BROWN COMPANY PUBLISHERS
Dubuque, Iowa

Contents

Preface

This is a book to be written in—that is why the outside margins are wider than usual. Read it with a pencil in your hand and write comments, notes, or jot down questions as you go along. Start now if you wish.

The readings in this book were selected to be discussed. That is why your notes are important. They will help you talk about the material you have read. Your opinion of these readings selections is important—what you think about them, whether you agree or disagree, and whether they have any meaning to you as a future teacher.

At the University of Texas at Austin these materials are used along with individual proctoring sessions. The student reads a section and then has an opportunity to discuss it with his proctor, another student who has previously completed the course. But these materials do not have to be used only in this way. They can serve as the basis for class discussion, for talks with the instructor, or even "bull sessions" among students. How you do it is not important; it is important that you think about and discuss the contents of these pages. This is the basis on which the readings were selected—to stimulate thought and discussion, perhaps even controversy.

Being a teacher is important; it requires skill and knowledge. It also requires understanding—understanding of yourself, of children, and of the world in which we live. This book is intended to help you gain this understanding.

All the readings in this collection stand or fall on their own merits. It is up to you to decide what "the point" to each of them is. In fact, you may find some of them pointless. This does not mean that you have "missed the point." All it means is that only you can judge what is relevant *to you*. Along the same lines, should a unifying theme emerge from your reading, hold onto it—it's yours.

Austin, Texas

L.F.S.N.
C.F.H.

Introduction

What happens when a teacher interacts with students in a classroom is hardly definable. Usually, that teacher has a command of
certain information in a subject area; that teacher also has a command of certain techniques which structure the interactions with
students concerning the subject-area information. Although both information and techniques may be standardized in a teacher preparation program, a teacher's meeting these standards does not guarantee
his effectiveness in a classroom. What makes teacher-student interaction undefinable and prevents the unqualified success of teacher
preparation programs is that a teacher is a person.

Often the person a teacher is, the qualities that give him his individuality and make him different from anyone else, determines his
effectiveness. When a teacher interacts with students, he interacts
primarily as a person and only secondarily in his role as a teacher. His
characteristic way of interacting, of communicating the subject-area
information, and of implementing teaching techniques sometimes is
the most important thing students can learn. In fact, the teacher as
the person his students see often prevents their learning anything
else. In a teacher's coming to understand himself, in his becoming a
person, he comes to be a more effective teacher.

1. Intensive Individualization of Teacher Preparation[1]

Frances F. Fuller

Almost everyone who will ever occupy a bed in a mental hospital was once in some teacher's first grade. So was every physicist and poet; every healer, murderer, pusher, and priest. Through the hands and minds and feelings of teachers pass all our children. In the face of such opportunity, what is the teacher's task in mental health? What, in fact, *is* mental health? How can a researcher or a teacher think about mental health?

Mental health can be thought of as subjective well being, as feeling good. But many great men did not feel good and were often racked by pain both physical and psychic.

Is mental health the absence of unconscious conflict, something a psychologist must define? No, it is not, for often productive, functioning men produce the same kinds of test protocols as hospitalized psychotics.

Mental health then is more than the absence of illness, more than well being, more even than joyfulness. We have conceived of it here as the developing capacity to *cope*. In behavior, it is successive hypothesis testing: marshalling one's resources to make a guess, trying out the guess, listening for results, using the results as new information to make a new guess, then trying that out. Mental health is this kind of going on as opposed to giving up.

Forty-Sixth Yearbook, *Mental Health and Teacher Education*, 1967. Reprinted with permission of the Association for Student Teaching, 1201 Sixteenth St., N.W., Washington, D.C. and Frances Fuller.

[1] This article is an excerpt from a longer report on the Texas Project, in which intensive study was made of the student-teacher preparation program at The University of Texas at Austin.

The teacher's job in mental health is to expand each child's ability to cope. How can he do that? This is one way:

> The student teacher and her supervisor had watched and discussed the short sound film of the student teacher teaching. The supervisor asked why one boy brightened up after an inaudible conversation with the student teacher. The student teacher said, "He hardly ever takes an interest. Everyone's about given up on him. I walked back to his table because he was drawing something while the class was doing arithmetic. He said the drawing was a test tube. We'd had a science lesson that morning, and I could hardly believe it, but he must have gotten interested in the test tubes." The supervisor asked her, "What did you do?" "Oh, I gave him a *bigger piece of paper*."

Sometimes a teacher can help a child develop the ability to cope by seeing the child's act as it is meant, by getting behind his eyes. A psychotherapist might smile about the symbolism of the test tube and the teacher's easy encouragement of a small boy's wanting to enlarge it. But all that can be skipped; this teacher did not need to know that impotence and underachievement are hypothesized to be related. He did know that a child can start to want to learn to cope; a simple act can help; the act can be as homely as giving him a bigger piece of paper.

Sometimes a supervisor can help a *teacher* develop his ability to cope.

> Student Teacher: (talking steadily) I'm doing just what I said I'd do—talk, talk, talk, talk, talk. A motor mouth. How can I quit it?
>
> Supervisor: Why try to quit? Could you make your talking more effective? (Silence) Don't talk less. Make it better. (Silence)
>
> Student Teacher: I never thought of that. (Long silence)

Just as the test tube found a bigger piece of paper, so the "motor mouth" might find a "bigger piece of paper," too—a larger scope instead of a smaller tongue. He might be helped to make both his talking and his listening more effective rather than to be advised to quit talking, which he probably couldn't do even if he tried. More important perhaps than the talking symptom, is someone's attempt to improve, rather than eliminate a part of him. Having experienced, himself, acceptance aimed at enhancing his ability to cope, he may be better able to accept limitations in others; to appreciate rather than eliminate children's differences; to enlarge, not desiccate, their powers.

Basic Premises

The following are five premises stemming from two orientations of the Texas Project: one being that of developmental-social psychology and the other being akin to the Rogerian approach to counseling.

The first was that the teacher's primary job is to maximize significant or experiential learning in students, i.e., learning which makes a difference in the individual's behavior.

A second premise was that teachers teach far more than just intellectual content in their total interactions with students. Students learn from teacher's attitudes and ways of responding which comprise part of their ability to cope, but which teachers may not be conscious of teaching. Whether there is, in the strict sense, incidental or unintentional, learning is an as yet unanswered question.[2] There seems to be little doubt, however, that there is incidental teaching. To adapt an adage, oftimes what teachers *are* speaks so loudly that students cannot hear what they say.

A third premise was that changing what the teaching does involves more than changing what the *teacher* does. If changes are to occur in what teaching does (i.e., in students' experiential learning) changes need to occur *in teachers* too; in how they think, feel, and respond, as well as in what they know; in short, in *their*, the teachers', experiential learning. If this is so, the teacher preparation institution's primary job is to maximize experiential learning for prospective teachers.

A fourth premise was that selected psychological assessment techniques can be helpful in understanding prospective teachers as individuals.

A fifth premise was that personal growth is facilitated by the presence of a serious meaningful problem and by

---

[2] Barry McLaughlin, " 'Intentional' and 'Incidental' Learning in Human Subjects." *Psychological Bulletin* 63: 359-376, 1965.

a therapist who is congruent, accepting, and empathically understanding. Ways were sought to create for prospective teachers (and ultimately, for children who are their students) a climate with the same meaning that a therapeutic climate, a climate facilitating personal growth, holds for clients. The therapeutic skills of listening, of discovering the client's concerns and perceptions, and of empathizing can contribute to the creation of such a climate in the classroom.

Vantage Points for Understanding

Psychological understanding of teacher preparation requires at least three vantage points.

One is the point of view of the teacher educator—the teacher preparation institution, the university supervisor, the public school supervising teacher, and all the professional persons involved in teacher preparation. This point of view is well represented, even over-represented. Most teacher preparation programs and most texts for prospective teachers, although attempting to consider the problem from the student's point of view, are based primarily on guesses by teacher educators about the prospective teacher's concerns and tasks.

A second vantage point required is one behind the eyes, between the ears, inside the viscera of the prospective teacher himself.

A third vantage point is that of some omniscient observer—all seeing, all hearing, all instituting—who can with perfect accuracy, art and resonance, reflect all the events seen and unseen of the classroom and the school: the precise moment a child first feels that math is hard or reading sissy; the teacher's glance that fires a first faint impulse to choose ulcers as a favored symptom; the sudden secret knowledge of power; the rapture of first communion with a word; all the trillion, trillion messages received and sent each day in school.

Through the Eyes of Prospective Teachers

The tremendous psychological complexity of teacher preparation, and especially of student teaching as it was communicated by students in the midst of it, almost defies description except in the words of the students themselves. These words come from many sources: from the typescripts of tape recordings of three semesters of weekly counseling-oriented, student teaching seminars,[3] from near-verbatim accounts by psychologists of over two hundred hour-long confidential "depth" interviews with student teachers before and after student teaching, from the case notes of therapists' "test interpretation" or counseling conferences and from tape recordings of many informal contacts between psychologists or curriculum supervisors and prospective teachers while the latter exploded, whispered, cried, smarted, gloated, beamed, or fussed over their most recent encounters with teaching. Currently a stimulated recall method, after Bloom,[4] is being used to investigate more systematically covert concerns and perceptions. For this purpose, student teachers watching a film of themselves teaching a class, attempt to recall their feelings, thoughts, expectations, and perceptions while teaching.

Composition of the Sample

The words that follow as examples come from some of almost one thousand students, primarily young women between the ages of nineteen and twenty-six and, except where noted, these are their concerns, their perceptions of a teacher's developmental tasks.

The composition of the sample is important. For example, one freshman education course was labeled completely useless by well over 90 per cent of all the student teachers seen in a confidential post-student-teaching interview, but it was judged brilliant, deep, enlightening by a selected subsample. The subsample

---

[3] Frances F. Fuller and Oliver H. Brown, "Counseling and Co-Counseling Student Teacher Groups." (Paper delivered at annual meeting of the American Psychological Association.) *American Psychologist* 19:457, 1964. (Abstract).

[4] Benjamin S. Bloom, "The Thought Processes of Students in Discussion." *Accent on Teaching.* Sidney J. French. (Editor). New York: Harper and Brothers, 1954.

was composed of student teachers over thirty-five: retired men, foreign students, musicians, artists, housewives, and other mature persons returning to college for certification. The context of these interviews indicates that the young inexperienced majority was unable to formulate the questions the course was designed to answer and only this young majority termed the course irrelevant, or, less elegantly, "mickey mouse."

Three arbitrary divisions will be made in reporting prospective teachers' experiences: (1) the concerns of student teachers as they progressed through their first semester of teaching in public schools, (2) their developmental tasks as they saw them, and (3) their reported and observed responses to these tasks. It should be noted that in reality, however, these comfortably neat divisions were neither neat nor comfortable, but more typically a flowing, intermingling, often baffling, whole.

Concerns of Student Teachers

In order to secure frank statements from student teachers about their real concerns as these developed through the student teaching experience, it was necessary to create an environment which they perceived as appropriate for free expression.

A prior review of the case notes of approximately two hundred confidential depth exit interviews with individual graduating student teachers in this population had indicated that student teaching was generally regarded as crucial and often stressful, that student teachers rarely voiced their failures, and that a protected but purposeful environment would be necessary to insure honest self-report.

Dr. Geneva Pilgrim had suggested that student teaching seminars, already a part of teacher preparation, become "counseling-oriented" seminars.

Discovering concerns of student teachers had not been the original or even the principal purpose for conducting the seminars. The main purpose had been to discover how to apply group therapy techniques to an ongoing program of teacher preparation. Lumpkin and McGuire had reported it feasible and accepted by volunteer student teachers when conducted outside the college program.[5]

In order to provide units for analysis, complete typescripts of tape recordings of seminars were divided into "communications" and these units were classified into thirteen categories. The arbitrary names given these categories were student teachers' concern with: Curriculum, Discipline, Grading and Evaluation, Parents of Pupils, Peers, Psychological Approaches to Teaching, Public School Situation, Pupils, Research Project, Routine, Self-Attitudes, Supervising Teachers, University.

Concerns classified were not necessarily the most obvious topic of the student teacher's statement in the seminar. When considered in context, the event or topic mentioned was often merely a vehicle for conveying an underlying concern. It was the *underlying* concern which was of interest in this analysis. A verbatim comment by a student teacher may illustrate the difference. The teacher here may seem to be talking about the tedium of teaching spelling:

> I got so blasted ego-involved and I wanted to do something sooo meaningful, and then to get up there and teach those stupid spelling words! There's nothing wrong with it. It's not that. But it was so flat.

Teaching spelling was, in context, not really central. Even the implied condemnation of a system which killed enthusiasm was incidental. Her underlying concern was her own disappointment.

From inspection of category frequencies, a pattern of concerns became apparent during the first seminar which was repeated in broad outline during the two succeeding semesters. During the early part of the semester, student teachers' concerns centered on themselves, and, as the semester advanced, they became more concerned with their pupils.

The earliest concerns of student teachers were almost disregarded by us during early seminars as mere concern

---

[5]Joseph H. Lumpkin, Jr., *Group Counseling and the Learning of Teacher Roles.* Unpublished Doctoral Dissertation. Austin: The University of Texas, 1954.

with routine and unrelated to the "real" business of teaching. Student teachers were eager to learn what school and class they were assigned to, who would ride in their car pool, the name of their supervisor and above all the public school supervising teacher to whom they would be assigned. It was during this period that they were most vividly aware of themselves and least aware of their pupils. When they did become aware of pupils, it was with a jaundiced eye, often seeing pupils as no more than potential "discipline" problems.

When the problem of control was resolved, and pupils could be seen as individuals, awareness of self began to be replaced by awareness of others. Student teachers gradually became less aware of themselves and more aware of their pupils. What they were teaching became of less concern than what pupils were really learning. It seemed that when the individual student teacher became more secure, it became possible for him to consider the welfare of others. As one student teacher put it, "When we have the class under control, that's our food and shelter."

Some student teachers never got enough "food and shelter" and, still cold and hungry, were unable to share the later concerns of their more fortunate friends. Such self-protecting student teachers typically avoided subsequent discussion of their own personal attitudes and values and the influences of these upon communication of subject matter, discussions to which student teachers advanced who had resolved problems of self-adequacy. Such self-concerned student teachers frequently changed the subject, introduced incidents others felt irrelevant, "forgot" or lost the trend of the conversation, sat silent, or otherwise avoided discussion of the more advanced concerns.

Stages of Concerns

Six stages of concerns emerged from the seminars. They were:

Stage One: Where do I stand?

Here student teachers were concerned with the coming student teaching situation and with their position in it. They were literally sitting on the edges of their chairs waiting to find out about their assignments, the school, the grade level, the supervising teacher, the university supervisor, the rules of the school, the orientation of the principal, and especially the expectations of supervising teachers, the requirements of the task and the limitations, both verbalized and tacit, upon them.

> S.T. 1: I don't know. I mean is it going to be my class? Or is it going to be the teacher's class? Can I teach what I want to, really? Can I try out new things?
> S.T. 2: Does she tell you what to do? Or can you make up your mind?
> S.T. 3: And what if she doesn't approve of the way I'm doing it?
> S.T. 1: And that's not all of it. I can't put my finger on it.
> S.T. 2: Oh, I think the anticipation—knowing the action is actually coming.
> S.T. 3: The big day when the bomb will fall.

When assignments have been made, the problem of discerning real expectations, the behaviors for which real rewards are given as opposed to those which just get lip service, the search for the real power structure, has just begun. Things are not always what they seem:

> S.T. 1: My supervising teacher is so good. She gives them a free rein. But she has them under perfect control.
> S.T. 2: They feel free with her. They just don't dare *not* to discuss.
> S.T. 1: Well, they get an "F" if they don't.

Even when the facts are plain, knowing where one stands is hard:

> S.T. 1: (Excitedly) I went to a conference with a mother today. It was actually a mother.
> S.T. 2: A real mother!
> S.T. 1: Mrs. M. said we are not student teachers, we are real teachers. (Pause) I sat there and didn't say a word. But they talk to you as well as the teacher.

In one school, student teachers reported being criticized as "unprofessional" because they avoided the teachers' lounge; and in another, the telephone as well as the lounge were explicitly forbidden them. One principal felt that student teachers who sent pupils to his office for punishment were abdicating their responsibility; another backed them up and even invited them to witness the paddling. If they ignored noisy members of another class in the hall, they might be judged irresponsible; if they took action, they might be told to stop "interfering." Even worse, the children might ignore *them*. Evaluating the subtle cues on which such judgments could be based called for social sophistication and sometimes two-faced inconsistency. Many otherwise committed, knowledgeable student teachers couldn't— or wouldn't—"play it smart."

Stage Two: How Adequate Am I?

This was another self-preservation phase. One concern was with subject matter adequacy. What do you do when a child asks about the past tense of "lie" and "lay" when this is something you've never been clear about yourself? What will the class think when you have to say, not the first or fourth, but the tenth time, "I don't know" or "Let's look that up."

A second, and overriding concern was class control. This is, of course, no surprise to anyone who has supervised student teachers. As hunters discuss the chase and sailors the shipwreck, student teachers from K through 12, but particularly in junior high school, talk about "discipline." Resolution of the need, on one hand, to be liked by pupils and, on the other, to frustrate their impulses in the interests of socialization, caused discomfort to most student teachers. For some, however, attempts at class control were deeply traumatic. For a student teacher who was a lonely only child, "discipline" meant alienating potential "playmates" in the class or even brothers and sisters whose late arrival made them more precious still. For the rebel, class control was "going over to the enemy." Unconsciously hostile student teachers sometimes panicked in fear of their own rage; passive ones cried; narcissistic ones were titillated and manipulated.

Discipline in student teaching is vastly complicated by the presence of a supervising teacher. First, his standards, if even slightly different regarding tolerable noise level and impulse expression, add another dimension to an already complex situation. More important, his aims and those of the student teacher are at odds: the teacher's aim is success; the student teacher needs the freedom to fail. As one so vividly documented it, they certainly can muff:

> I cannot control them at all. They do everything they can to tease me. They take the little slips I have to send to the office. Then I have to hunt for them. They finally give them back. And they run around the room. Yes, they do.

Their repertoire of "staring them down," snapping fingers, making pupils "freeze," writing names on the board and so on, works only temporarily. Remaining in control is more complex than merely keeping order.

The view that "discipline problems," like a fever, are merely a symptom was relatively infrequent. Discipline problems were initially treated as discrete events susceptible of cure by prescription, although the "symptom" hypothesis was given lip service. The reason for this seemed to be that once class control was seen as a product of emotional interaction between teacher and class, what the teacher *is* (and cannot change quickly, if at all) instead of what the teacher *does*, is subject to inspection. So are many values of doubtful lineage, unexamined feelings, shaky convictions. In the area of discipline, it is not possible to abstain. Doing nothing is always doing something.

Stage Three: Why Do They Do That?

At this stage, student teachers were concerned with individual students, generally the "problem" students and their strange behavior. They saw masochistic behavior:

> But I can't give her the scissors. The others cut the paper, but she just sits and slices little pieces off her fingers.

And fear:

> I know how his father looks to him—like a great big ogre. I don't blame him for lying to his father about me, but what am I going to tell the father when he comes to see me?

Or withdrawal:

> She's no trouble, but so strange—just not there at all.

Children disdain them:

> When I said who I hoped would win the fight, I heard this one little boy say, "Nigger lover." I didn't know what to say.

Or take up arms against them:

> She doesn't like me and she is arousing the others against me.

Occasionally, the problem resides entirely within a child too troubled for any teacher's help. But more often it is the teacher's own feelings about the child which are troublesome, not the child's feelings about himself. To resolve this concern, more than knowledge of "child psychology" is required. A revision in the teacher's attitude as well as an addition to the teacher's knowledge is necessary.

Stage Four: How Do You Think I'm Doing?

During this stage, some students merely worried about their student teaching grade, but most tried to discern how parents, supervising teachers, principals, and others were evaluating them. Sometimes such an evaluation was crucial:

> I won't apply if I don't have a chance. I know you shouldn't be grade conscious, but what if I make a C? If I did, I wouldn't go on teaching.

Important as they are, dependable evaluations seem hard to get:

> Today I had a parent come down and complain about me. Yesterday he acted lovely to me and today he is talking to Miss S.

Even principals can be distrusted if they try too hard to be agreeable:

> The principal came in and said I did a wonderful job. I guess he liked the way I took roll. [Laughter] Then when he left he said to Mrs. M., "What is her name?" [Laughter] And I have to have his recommendation!

It is hard to ask frankly for honest evaluation:

> S.T. : The only thing Dr. T. said to me was, "L., if your lesson plans were a little more detailed I could help you." Of course, he was standing there with one tiny little piece of my notebook paper. [Laughs almost hysterically.] If

he had only said, "Now look, you've got to get busy."
[Bangs on table to imitate fantasied supervisor gesture.]
Of course I'm asking to be babied. [Laughs] But if he
smiles I just sit there and tell him stories about what
happened and we have a good old time. I hope I'm not
going to get slapped in the face at the end of the course.
Counselor: You mean the babying may stop all of a sudden?
S.T. : Golly, yes. I said to my supervising teacher, "Has he
said anything to you?"

Stage Five: How Are They Doing?

At this stage student teachers were concerned about
what the pupils they taught were actually learning as
distinguished from what they believed themselves to be
teaching. In our early seminars, student teachers rarely
asked the question, "Will the class remember that?" Although they often discussed with their supervisors outside the seminar the responses their classes made, and
even devoted considerable time to an evaluation of what
learning had taken place, this question was not raised
spontaneously by the student teachers themselves in the
early seminars.

Student teachers obviously knew in an intellectual
way at least that evaluating what their pupils were learning was important in the eyes of their university supervisors. This became apparent when a university supervisor unknowingly set off a near panic by suggesting
immediately before the start of a counseling seminar
that she would like the student teachers to reflect in
their lesson plans the provisions they were making for
individual differences among their junior high pupils and
for evaluating the individual learning which took place.

As she spoke, the student teachers rapidly made
notes, and when she asked if there were questions, there
was one about the form this was to take. The university
supervisor left and, as soon as the door closed, there was
a loud explosion of comments:

Several: What did she mean? Someone run after her. [Some-
one started out the door]
S.T. 1: (Shouting over the din) Wait a minute! Maybe we can
figure this out!
S.T. 2: What did she mean about individualizing your lesson
plans?
S.T. 3: I think she meant individual levels.

S.T. 1: I don't think she meant that although we've been talking about it in here. I think maybe that I have not
been applying theory. I mean I have given a lot of
individual attention without their knowing it. [Illus-
trates by recounting an incident from her class.]

S.T. 4: I think that is what she means but in the plan, not in
just telling the child, but on a mass level of individual
attention and planning. For example, a variety of
assignments. Since you have a feeling of confidence
now about the mechanics of teaching, start putting
more time in on the planning. Is that what she means?

S.T. 5: Yes, that makes sense.

S.T. 4: Before we looked up and saw a sea of faces and you
could just tell when someone was eating candy or the
main thing was when someone wasn't working. Now
we can change the lesson or explain it more thoroughly and look out for individuals more than just
getting the work done.

Stage Six: Who Am I?

From the first, many *unconscious* interactions, between student teachers and their pupils, were apparent
to the counselor. The impact one student teacher had
on her pupils would often be apparent to some of the
others in the seminar, but not to the student teacher
herself. In an early meeting, for example, one student
teacher had a "minor discipline problem."

S.T. 1: I say, "Yes, that's your homework." Then they wave
their hands to ask questions and they let "Mama" slip
out.

Several: They really do?

S.T. 1: And I say! Imagine! Thirteen years old!

S.T. 2: You mean they know they're doing it?

S.T. 1: Maybe some of them do. But I can remember when I
was in grade school, I used to let "Mama" slip out all
the time.

S.T. 2: Yes, but not in high school!

At a later meeting:

Counselor: Do they still call you "Mama?"

S.T. 1: No, they've grown up all of a sudden.

Several: *They* have?

S.T. 1: Well, *they* were the ones that were calling me
"Mama." (Laughs) I wasn't calling *them*. No, but really,
they've quit calling me "Mama." One even asked what
my married name would be.

At the last meeting of the group, without referring to the "Mama" incident, Student Teacher 1 said: "Oh, I know me—I'm the mother hen."

The group knew, if she did not, that what she *was*, a "Mama hen," spoke so loudly to the class that they could not hear her tell them *not* to call her "Mama." They were rather like the little girl who was cautioned not to look at the enormous nose of the distinguished visitor. When she took his proffered gift, she said, eyes carefully averted, "Thank you, Mr. Nose."

To know oneself requires first deciding how much self-knowledge one can bear.

> S.T. 1: How much do I want to know about myself? [Long silence] I don't know. [She expresses doubts about her qualifications for teaching.]
>
> S.T. 2: It makes me feel sad.
>
> S.T. 3: I feel we want to keep her [S.T. 1] in as a teacher, but more important, we want to get her *found.* I mean if she decided right now she wanted to be a doctor instead of a teacher and she was just very sure, I don't think any of us would be sad. It is just that uncertainty.
>
> S.T. 2: Well the reason I feel sad when she was saying that was because I have had feelings identical to those, except that I just happen to be more a conformist than you are, so I just pushed all my fears and doubts away. (Softly) So when you say that—well, I am sad because it makes mine come back.
>
> S.T. 1: Do you want yours to come back?
>
> S.T. 2: (Very softly) No, I don't want them to come back. But, I really am proud of you for standing up and saying, "Well, I'm not sure."

Teachers' Concerns and Teachers' Tasks

A pattern approximating this six stage sequence cropped up not only in other seminars which followed but in the case notes of interviews with scores of student teachers.

These stages were considered sufficiently important to become one basis for selecting content and procedures for instruction of prospective teachers. Their concerns were considered important for two reasons.

First, the path from knowledge of subject matter to communication of subject matter is not simple and direct but complex and devious. The proponents of scholarship alone as preparation for teaching are doomed to empirical embarrassment simply because persons and, of course, teachers, are not fixed ratio input-output mechanisms, but rather jungles of intervening, and interfering or facilitating, variables. One simple-minded but powerful class of variables is the teacher's own needs and concerns. Before pupils' interests and needs could be sensed by the student teacher, his own most pressing needs had to be satisfied.

Second, the student teacher's stage of concern emerged as a rough index of his readiness to learn to teach. A student teacher preoccupied with a defiant child rarely could internalize instruction by university supervisors about teaching concepts, for example, no matter how many lesson plans he wrote. Too, his stage of concern indicated to some extent how he felt *while* teaching, how much he was able to learn and change in the actual classroom situation.

When the events observed in classrooms of student teachers were compared with their statements in seminar, the statements usually jibed with the *facts*, but there were wide differences between the *covert experience* as it was revealed by the student teacher in the seminar and his or her *overt behavior* while teaching. Students varied tremendously in their ability or willingness to appear more confident than they felt, to channel anxiety, and particularly to persevere.

These differences seemed due, in part at least, to the individual student teacher's life situation and his consequent need to teach. Lower class men and women, for whom teaching was a step up the social ladder, admitted fewer problems to their university supervisors than to counselors. So did newly married girls under pressure to put a husband through graduate school, and duller students less likely to find opportunities outside teaching. In brief, highly motivated students could mask felt inadequacies. As a consequence, the more likely the student teacher was to remain in the profession and the more he needed help, the less likely he was to seek it except in counseling sessions. The students said, "Don't tell your supervisor what you are really wondering because then you won't get a good grade."

Developmental Tasks of Student Teachers

Developmental tasks related to each concern were defined as follows:

1. The concerns of the first stage, finding security in the total school situation, seem to involve the abilities to explore the physical plant freely; to discover with some degree of certainty what school policies are regarding such things as conferences with parents, administration of punishment, and handling emergencies; to estimate the amount of support which can be expected from the school principal and other supervisors in a great variety of situations; to build working relationships with other teachers; to utilize school resources such as audio-visual aids, libraries, visiting teachers, and community counseling services; in general to determine the limits of their acceptance as professional persons in halls, cafeteria, library, playground, teacher's lounge, and principal's office.

2. Feeling secure with one's class seems to involve the ability to understand and explain subject matter, to answer pupils' questions, to say "I don't know," to have the freedom to fail on occasion; to mobilize resources and make effective changes when failures reoccur; to master the fear that students will hang from the chandeliers, climb out the windows, or merely refuse to cooperate; to catch an eye, give a warning glance or an approving nod without missing a beat; to feel bigger and stronger than the children if only because society has designated the teacher as its representative; to speak clearly, to be understood; to make out schedules, to estimate the time required to finish assignments; to anticipate problems peculiar to the social class, pecking order, habits, expectations, or just plain idiosyncracies of this particular class; to locate objects; in general to create an atmosphere in which teaching is possible, as distinguished from minding children or merely playing with them.

3. Coping with individual children seems to involve the abilities to establish behavior norms; to sense what is usual, what is strange; to interpret test scores, clinical write-ups and a variety of data such as that in permanent record folders; to master the anxiety aroused by

the pitiful child and the whole gamut of emotions aroused in a teacher by children's unstinting acceptance, brutal honesty, and amoral disregard for propriety; to decide how to react to the boy who cries for hours, the girl who is forever bruised, burned, or bandaged, the small boy who pats her posterior, or the bigger one who mutters aft, "I wish I had a swing like that in my back yard"; to do something with the child who lies, fights, or urinates in the classroom; to talk to parents in person or on the phone; to differentiate behavior which is the child's reaction to himself, from that which is his reaction to his teacher; to understand that doing nothing is usually doing something. Even more, it seems to include the ability of the teacher to estimate his own differential impact on different children, to realize that the very same act may have one effect on one child and a very different effect on another child.

4. and 5. Concern with supervisors' evaluations of the student teachers seems only to be resolved when stage 4 and stage 5 concerns are merged, for they must be able to evaluate their own teaching product, and this in turn requires that they be able to estimate the effect their teaching has had on students. Evaluation involves a willingness to ask and then to hold still and listen; to take into account and to partial out the biases and prejudices of those who are responsible for evaluation; to evolve at least short term goals for themselves and their classes; to devise measures both formal and informal which will estimate the effects of what they have done; to attend to those estimates; to understand that estimate is not measurement, and finally to react constructively by trying new procedures, rather than blaming someone else or giving up.

6. The stage six developmental concern "Who am I?" could not be operationally defined with the early seminar groups since too few student teachers were then sufficiently secure in all the preceding developmental tasks to address themselves to this question in the context of their public school teaching.[6]

[6]Later in the study it was possible to state stage six developmental tasks in student-teacher terms. Some statements of the students at stages five and six can be subsumed under eight preliminary categories:

1. *Taking into account the characteristics and learning capacities of the class.*
   It bothers me when I forget they are in fourth grade.
   I want them to like everything.
   I work on phrasing questions so they'll answer with new ideas.
   The record folders in the office only go so far—not far enough at all.

2. *Specifying objectives in teaching content.*
   The thing with me is to get them to see the whole picture, not just one part.
   My worst problem is that I need some big direction.
   They need generalizations bigger than those I have myself.

3. *Specifying one's own limitations.*
   I talk too much instead of letting them experience it themselves.
   All I can hear is the criticism. If she says one small thing is wrong, I feel as though she said the whole thing is wrong.
   I have that kind of face. If I'm not stonefaced at first, I can't tighten up later.
   I had to have someone baby me then or I'd have quit teaching.

4. *Partializing out one's own contributions to difficulties.*
   Mrs S. says it is her worst, most diverse class in eleven years, but I have the problem of knowing when I can be free with them and when not.
   I call that type "smart alecks" to myself, so you can tell I have a personal problem with them.

5. *Trying out new ways and accepting the discomfort that* may *accompany change.*
   Working in committees is frustrating to me but helpful to them.
   Letting them walk around bugs me because I never could do it.
   These children demand to be taught as individuals and that is hard, but I see what it's like to teach a different way.

6. *Evaluating one's effectiveness in terms of children's gain.*
   How can we rate ourselves until we see how much they have retained?
   Seeing a face light up like he's got it is the best reward.
   I know and the children know, so what if she (the supervisor) *doesn't* stop by.

7. *Relating to and evaluating supervisors as colleagues.*
   We combined forces. She gives me ideas and I give her ideas.
   She snaps at me, but even her husband tells her he's not a mind reader.

8. *Selecting a teaching job considering what one has to give as well as get.*
   I'm no scholar. I'm just a nice guy. That school is in the poorest section, but it's got a market for nice guys.
   I'm only applying to private schools. I would not like lower class students and I'm sure they'd know it.

The author selects the following two kinds of classroom incidents for inclusion in teacher preparation programs: coping teacher behavior and problem teacher behavior.

Coping Teacher Behavior

One kind of coping response was the *insightful pairing of instructional method and pupils' needs.*

> Juan is nine and still in second grade. His parents are migrant farm workers. He tries to read but only produces a sing-song chant of indistinguishable sounds. When the student teacher introduced addition, he called answers so fast that no one else got a chance and he set up a howl when the lesson was over. He's counted many baskets of beans. His student teacher gave him written word problems in arithmetic, first mostly numbers, and now is gradually increasing the proportion of words to numbers in his assignments.

Student teachers used instructional material and procedures to help them handle diverse problems, sometimes in ways reminiscent of bibliotherapy and other times of play therapy: fictional heroes at once intellectual and masculine for the boy who thought reading sissy; a chance to paint the sky in swooping sweeps for the anxious, clumsy, tense aggressor; a speaking part behind a mask for the shy child.

Another kind of coping response utilized *instruction to turn problems into opportunities.*

> Right after the smoke bomb went off, the assistant principal came to the door to collect the absence slips. Some boys were rolling on the floor coughing and the girls were letting out little screeches. Of course, first I had to get them out of there to be sure everyone was O.K. Afterward, we got interested in the thing and did an experiment on the effects of that kind of gas on human tissue.

This student teacher was more concerned with protecting the class than with protecting herself. When this same incident was included in a free response pencil and paper instrument, many teacher responses were self-protective, punitive, passive, or just exasperated: "Explain to the principal it wasn't my fault." "Punish the ringleaders." "Punish the whole class." "Send them to the office." "Boys will be boys." "Laugh at the ridiculousness of it."

Another way of coping was *the search for relevant information.* Teachers sometimes used pupils' poetry, art, and other class work for this purpose, much as psychologists use projective data. Some understood the language of emotions:

> He actually threw it at me! I was so scared I shook for a week. Then yesterday I read what he wrote. [To psychologist] You'll LOVE this. We were studying seeds, and they all wrote, if I were a seed. He said [Holds up a large wide-lined rough sheet] "I am a watermelon. I am going to be eaten. I am cut. I am screaming. All my pink is running out. Even if they cut me, I am not good. I am calling, calling. Goodbye." [There was a gasp from the seminar.] When I read that, I thought, he feels like he's coming apart. (She cupped her hands as though to scoop him up.) He *needs* me to hold him together. And I'm not afraid of him any more. [At a later session] Well, I don't know if he's any better, but I know *I am,* and so is the class.

Students' art work often communicated to their teachers their perceptions of themselves, of their school, their tasks, their world. Some teachers asked pupils to draw self-portraits or respond to music with drawings, poems or prose, and used these productions to make assignments, to divide students into groups, and to individualize instruction in many other ways.

Student teachers used new information to *formulate and test hypotheses.* Sometimes, as in the case above, the method was helpful with a single child, but it was also useful in parent conferences, group instruction, any situation that needed to be "researched."

Teachers often brought to bear on developing neurotic patterns their own healthy responses, much as therapists use themselves as instruments in therapy. For example, they sometimes reacted spontaneously against rewarding unhealthy behavior or punishing healthy behavior.

> Phil hardly ever says a word, just stares out the window. I let him be George Washington in the play because he only had to say one line and to shade his eyes to look across the Delaware. His mother came to see the play. At first, he just looked down, but then he said his line just like we practiced. I gave him a big smile. Then I noticed his mother crying! The better he did, the more she cried. [Pause] They weren't tears of joy, either. I think she must need *him* to need *her.* [Pause] I don't know what I'll *do.* But he's going to have *one* woman in his life who doesn't need him to be a baby. *Me.*

A lot of boys (and men!) need one woman in their lives who doesn't require them to be dependent or ineffectual; who appreciates their masculinity, and can socialize it without hostility; and who can understand (not necessarily in words) that tenderness can be wedded to aggression without demasculinizing either. Like many other teachers, this one bypassed the psychological lingo: withdrawal, Oedipal conflict, impotence, underachievement. She acted on a basic, healthy notion that, though mothers love their children, to grow to manhood little boys need to learn to do things on their own. Most of all, she fully wanted little boys to be just what they are, little boys.

Another coping response seemed to be the *teacher's reliance on his or her own deepest feelings about what was possible for him in a given situation.* Here, student teachers' misperceptions about psychology were sometimes roadblocks. Student teachers were sometimes surprised to discover that behavior they considered psychologically disapproved but their "last resort" was not disapproved at all. Their surprise pointed up a frequent theme: the discrepancy between what they called "theory," (usually permissiveness) and application, i.e., what they felt they had to do, even if in secret, to survive. They often fought their most important battle for class control, and for their role as teacher, with what they considered illicit weapons. As one who did survive said, "I didn't want to hurt his little ego, but it was him or me."

Another positive response was *an unwillingness to become overcommitted emotionally, stemming from a knowledge of one's own limitations and resources.*

> She's so pitiful. Her mother works to support five of them and has no time for her. She asked me to take her home to be my little girl. I just ached. But I told her I couldn't take her home, but I loved to be her teacher and loved to see her every day. What I have to do is help her make good friends in the class.

The acknowledgment that others besides the teacher, especially agemates, can contribute to solutions was a coping response. Student teachers still concerned with their own security were most likely to think of the teacher as the only helping agent in the classroom.

Others could use pairing or grouping of children, socio-metric devices, extra-class and social activities, particularly in junior high and secondary school, to tap the rich resources of classmates.

Problem Teacher Behavior

Student teachers also responded to their tasks in ways which seemed to us damaging to children and sometimes to other persons. Rarely did this take the form of sarcasm or threats, never of physical cruelty. Instead, it was subtle, often even unconscious.

Student teachers sometimes responded negatively to incidents like those recounted above, or did not respond at all. They might demand what a pupil could not do and so discourage his trying at all; refuse to accept a small but maximum effort instead of rewarding it with a "bigger piece of paper"; increase frustration beyond the necessary minimum by placing unnecessary obstacles or proscriptions in the way, like holding to a lockstep the bright, curious, creative students; refuse release of insistent natural physical needs like the needs of primary children for activity after excitement; shame students without providing means of restitution; reward self-defeating behavior or punish coping responses. Rarely did a teacher know his behavior to be hostile. In this sense, destructive teaching is mainly "incidental," that is, related to limitations in capacity and unconsciously held attitudes.

Social class and sexual attitudes of which the teacher was not aware, were a frequent source of what seemed to be damaging teacher behavior. A fairly common example is the sixth grader or junior high school girl, precociously mature physically, but still a child inside, still in need of maternal affection but "too big" for it. She may elicit patient disdain from the women whose support and guidance she asks for in her backward, self-defeating way:

> S.T. 1: She's one of those—well, she's only thirteen, but she wears those cheap tight sweaters and gets up every five minutes to sharpen her pencil or something. She's always asking me, "Do you like the sorority house?" or some other silly question. But her last theme was the

end. She told about meeting some boys at night and then said her girl friend got very friendly with one boy. And then (reading from scrawled paper) she says, "They got very, very, very, very, *very* friendly."

S.T. 2: What's that you wrote there on it?

S.T. 1: Well, I knew I shouldn't be too hard on her. They're probably poor and all. So I just wrote in the margin *"NOT CLEAR."*

The pathos of a big bosomed child, using to gain affection the only thing she felt she had, her body, and naively reporting it to her glamorous student teacher in the hope she would impress her idol, was all lost on her student teacher. The student teacher admitted more of the truth than she knew when she wrote, "Not clear."

Sometimes unconsciously-held attitudes severely limited or distorted student teachers' perceptions of what was happening in the classroom. For example, student teachers reported that they had not "seen" children's masturbation in the classroom until it was pointed out to them, although they had been looking at it for several months. After it was pointed out, they would say they hadn't known what it was, or they hadn't stopped to think what it was or didn't "want" to see it.

Upwardly striving teachers reared in economically deprived families were sometimes hostile toward bright advantaged children who did not have to work as hard as their teachers had had to work. Children whose scholarly parents provided them with stimulating intellectual fare at home were sometimes barely tolerated by their limited—and limiting—teachers. Such teachers labeled these children "lazy." The children, bored, retaliated by misbehaving. When such a student teacher was assigned to a supervising teacher whose background was similarly limited, they could stand against the world together in their misguided righteousness, especially if they were both hard workers with good scholastic records.

Coping with Supervisors

Student teachers' greatest astuteness, best kept secrets, and most agonizing problems were reserved for their relationship with their university supervisors and supervising teachers. Most student teachers "played it smart," i.e., they adapted themselves to their supervisors when they could. When they sized up the supervisor as someone who needed to be needed, they were full of questions, needs, and gratitude, phoned him at home and dragged their tired bodies at semester's end to one last reunion. If the university supervisor was busy with a Ph.D. in process, they put on minutely planned teaching shows at school for his infrequent visits, kept a stiff upper lip in trouble and carried on alone or leaned on one another for support. They openly admitted competing with one another in their group meetings with their supervisor to give good reports of themselves and bring up only high status and interesting problems, rather than the dull, messy, or resistant ones.

Their relationship with their supervising teachers was almost unanimously conceded by graduating student teachers to be the single most critical experience in all their teaching preparation (and, we might say parenthetically, the least supported by teacher preparation institutions). Most student teachers who survived were well aware of their supervising teacher's covert attitudes toward them. If they were often sent out of the classroom for library books which were already in the classroom, they knew they were in the teacher's way. They demonstrated considerable skill in establishing relationships attuned to the supervising teacher's needs.

Even so, explosions occurred: Witness the pairing of Miss Mamie Goode, striving lower class supervising teacher, and Ann Van DeVee. Expensively dressed, full of stories of her European tour, a novelty, Ann flashed about the room, seducing the class, her principal, and her supervisor into pity and disdain for the brown-hen teacher who was, ultimately, held responsible for the class.

Such explosions were almost always the product of attitudes and values whose etiology, and sometimes even existence, was unconscious. Many such combinations were reported: the devotee of unpopular causes and the clucking homebound mama; the woolly psychoanalyzer and the well defended big-time-operator. A whole gamut of collisions was possible when total strangers were paired in this intimate relationship.

More often, though, there was no collision even when one seemed likely. When it was, the student teacher generally tried to absorb it. The most common consequence was an effort, often futile, by the student teacher to imitate his supervising teacher:

> Sobersided Prudence read to the class, from a collection of humor, the story "The Man Who Lost His Head." Her supervising teacher, a flamboyant woman, sat in the back gesticulating energetically, trying to help. Prudence tried to ham it up. It was an embarrassing failure. She was tense and gawky and the class lost interest. At the end, one boy asked, "Was it supposed to be funny?"

Even in routine matters like giving directions, student teachers often had to find their own idiosyncratic style:

> My supervising teacher can say "Take out your arithmetic books and work these problems" and they do. If I say that, there's bedlam. I have to say "Take out your pencil and nothing else" and wait until they do. Then, "Take out your book and nothing else" and wait. I don't know why it is, but what they do for me and what they do for her are just two different things.

In summary, the total task with which the prospective teacher is *concerned* is psychologically complex. But with some complexities many of them cannot be concerned, at least not deeply, such as those involved in the communication of varying content, in the reliable, valid measurement of effect, in their own real impact and their limitations. The sum of both is a towering task. As the plaques they frequently hung in their dorms put it, "Anyone who remains calm simply does not understand the situation."

2. Shooting an Elephant

George Orwell

In Moulmein, in Lower Burma, I was hated by large numbers of people—the only time in my life that I have been important enough for this to happen to me. I was sub-divisional police officer of the town, and in an aimless, petty kind of way anti-European feeling was very bitter. No one had the guts to raise a riot, but if a European woman went through the bazaars alone somebody would probably spit betel juice over her dress. As a police officer I was an obvious target and was baited whenever it seemed safe to do so. When a nimble Burman tripped me up on the football field and the referee (another Burman) looked the other way, the crowd yelled with hideous laughter. This happened more than once. In the end the sneering yellow faces of young men that met me everywhere, the insults hooted after me when I was at a safe distance, got badly on my nerves. The young Buddhist priests were the worst of all. There were several thousands of them in the town and none of them seemed to have anything to do except stand on street corners and jeer at Europeans.

All this was perplexing and upsetting. For at that time I had already made up my mind that imperialism was an evil thing and the sooner I chucked up my job and got out of it the better. Theoretically—and secretly, of course—I was all for the Burmese and all against their oppressors, the British. As for the job I was doing, I hated it more bitterly than I can perhaps make clear. In a job like that you see the dirty work of Empire at close quarters. The wretched prisoners huddling in the stinking cages of the lock-ups, the grey, cowed faces of the long-term convicts, the scarred buttocks of the men who had been flogged with bamboos—all these oppressed me with an intolerable sense of guilt. But I could get nothing into perspective. I was young and ill-educated and I had had to think out my problems in the utter silence that is imposed on every Englishman in the East. I did not even know that the British Empire is dying, still less did I know that it is a great deal better than the younger empires that are going to supplant it. All I knew was that I was stuck between my hatred of the empire I served and my rage against the evil-spirited little beasts who tried to make my job impossible. With one part of my mind I thought of the British Raj as an unbreakable tyranny, as something clamped down, in *saecula saeculorum,* upon the will of prostrate peoples; with another part I thought that the greatest joy in the world would be to drive a bayonet into a Buddhist priest's guts. Feelings like these are the normal by-products of imperialism; ask any Anglo-Indian official, if you can catch him off duty.

One day something happened which in a roundabout way was enlightening. It was a tiny incident in itself, but it gave me a better glimpse than I had had before of the real nature of imperialism—the real motives for which despotic governments act. Early one morning the sub-inspector at a police station the other end of the town rang me up on the phone and said that an elephant was ravaging the bazaar. Would I please come and do something about it? I did not know what I could do, but I wanted to see what was happening and I got on to a pony and started out. I took my rifle, an old .44 Winchester and much too small to kill an elephant, but I thought the noise might be useful *in terrorem.* Various Burmans stopped me on the way and told me about the elephant's doings. It was not, of course, a wild elephant, but a tame one which had gone "must". It had been chained up, as tame elephants always are when their attack of "must" is due, but on the previous night it had broken its chain and escaped. Its mahout, the only person who could manage it when it was in that state, had set out in pursuit, but had taken the wrong direction and was now twelve hours' journey away, and in the morning the elephant had suddenly reappeared in the town. The Burmese population had no weapons and were quite helpless against it. It had already destroyed somebody's bamboo hut, killed a cow and raided some fruit-stalls and devoured the stock; it also had met the municipal rubbish van and, when the driver jumped out and took to his heels, had turned the van over and inflicted violences upon it.

The Burmese sub-inspector and some Indian constables were waiting for me in the quarter where the elephant had been seen. It was a very poor quarter, a labyrinth of squalid bamboo huts, thatched with palm-leaf, winding all over a steep hillside. I remember that it was a cloudy, stuffy morning at the beginning of the rains. We began questioning the people as to where the elephant had gone and, as usual, failed to get any definite information. That is unvariably the case in the East; a story always sounds clear enough at a distance, but the nearer you get to the scene of events the vaguer it becomes. Some of the people said the elephant had gone in one direction, some said that he had gone in another, some professed not even to have heard of any elephant. I had almost made up my mind that the whole story was a pack of lies, when we heard yells a little distance away. There was a loud, scandalized cry of "Go away, child! Go away this instant!" and an old woman with a switch in her hand came round the corner of a hut, violently shooing away a crowd of naked children. Some more women followed, clicking their tongues and exclaiming; evidently there was something that the children ought not to have seen. I rounded the hut and saw a man's dead body sprawling in the mud. He was an Indian, a black Dravidian coolie, almost naked, and he could not have been dead many minutes. The people said that the elephant had come suddenly upon him round the corner of the hut, caught him with his trunk, put its foot on his back and ground him into the earth. This was the rainy season and the ground was soft, and his face had scored a trench a foot deep and a couple of yards long. He was lying on his belly with arms crucified and head sharply twisted to one side. His face was coated with mud, the eyes wide open, the teeth bared and grinning with an expression of unendurable agony. (Never tell me, by the way, that the dead look peaceful. Most of the corpses I have seen looked devilish.) The friction of the great beast's foot had stripped the skin from his back as neatly as one skins a rabbit. As soon as I saw the dead man I sent an orderly to a friend's house nearby to borrow an elephant rifle. I had already sent back the pony, not wanting it to go mad with fright and throw me if it smelt the elephant.

The orderly came back in a few minutes with a rifle and five cartridges, and meanwhile some Burmans had arrived and told us that the elephant was in the paddy fields below, only a few hundred yards away. As I started forward practically the whole population of the quarter flocked out of the houses and followed me. They had seen the rifle and were all shouting excitedly that I was going to shoot the elephant. They had not shown much interest in the elephant when he was merely ravaging their homes, but it was different now that he was going to be shot. It was a bit of fun to them, as it would be to an English crowd; besides, they wanted the meat. It made me vaguely uneasy. I had no intention of shooting the elephant—I had merely sent for the rifle to defend myself if necessary—and it is always unnerving to have a crowd following you. I marched down the hill, looking and feeling a fool, with the rifle over my shoulder and an ever-growing army of people jostling at my heels. At the bottom, when you got away from the huts, there was a metalled road and beyond that a miry waste of paddy fields a thousand yards across, not yet ploughed but soggy from the first rains and dotted with coarse grass. The elephant was standing eight yards from the road, his left side towards us. He took not the slightest notice of the crowd's approach. He was tearing up bunches of grass, beating them against his knees to clean them and stuffing them into his mouth.

I had halted on the road. As soon as I saw the elephant I knew with perfect certainty that I ought not

to shoot him. It is a serious matter to shoot a working
elephant—it is comparable to destroying a huge and
costly piece of machinery—and obviously one ought not
to do it if it can possibly be avoided. And at that
distance, peacefully eating, the elephant looked no more
dangerous than a cow. I thought then and I think now
that his attack of "must" was already passing off, in
which case he would merely wander harmlessly about
until the mahout came back and caught him. Moreover,
I did not in the least want to shoot him. I decided that I
would watch him for a little while to make sure that he
did not turn savage again, and then go home.

But at that moment I glanced around at the crowd
that had followed me. It was an immense crowd, two
thousand at the least and growing every minute. It
blocked the road for a long distance on either side. I
looked at the sea of yellow faces above the garish
clothes—faces all happy and excited over this bit of fun,
all certain that the elephant was going to be shot. They
were watching me as they would watch a conjurer about
to perform a trick. They did not like me, but with the
magical rifle in my hands, I was momentarily worth
watching. And suddenly I realized that I should have to
shoot the elephant after all. The people expected it of
me and I had got to do it; I could feel their two
thousand wills pressing me forward, irresistibly. And it
was at this moment, as I stood there with the rifle in my
hands, that I first grasped the hollowness, the futility of
the white man's dominion in the East. Here was I, the
white man with his gun, standing in front of the
unarmed native crowd—seemingly the leading actor of
the piece; but in reality I was only an absurd puppet
pushed to and fro by the will of those yellow faces
behind. I perceived in this moment that when the white
man turns tyrant it is his own freedom that he destroys.
He becomes a sort of hollow, posing dummy, the
conventionalized figure of a sahib. For it is the
condition of his rule that he shall spend his life in trying
to impress the "natives," and so in every crisis he has to
to do what the "natives" expect of him. He wears a
mask, and his face grows to fit it. I had got to shoot the
elephant. I had committed myself to doing it when I

sent for the rifle. A sahib has got to act like a sahib; he has got to appear resolute, to know his own mind and do definite things. To come all that way, rifle in hand, with two thousand people marching at my heels, and then to trail feebly away, having done nothing—no, that was impossible. The crowd would laugh at me. And my whole life, every white man's life in the East, was one long struggle not to be laughed at.

But I did not want to shoot the elephant, I watched him beating his bunch of grass against his knees, with that preoccupied grandmotherly air that elephants have. It seemed to me that it would be murder to shoot him. At that age I was not squeamish about killing animals, but I had never shot an elephant and never wanted to. (Somehow it always seems worse to kill a *large* animal.) Besides, there was the beast's owner to be considered. Alive, the elephant was worth at least a hundred pounds; dead, he would only be worth the value of his tusks, five pounds, possibly. But I had got to act quickly. I turned to some experienced-looking Burmans who had been there when we arrived, and asked them how the elephant had been behaving. They all said the same thing: he took no notice of you if you left him alone, but he might charge if you went too close to him.

It was perfectly clear to me what I ought to do. I ought to walk up to within, say, twenty-five yards of the elephant and test his behavior. If he charged, I could shoot; if he took no notice of me, it would be safe to leave him until the mahout came back. But also I knew that I was going to do no such thing. I was a poor shot with a rifle and the ground was soft mud into which one would sink at every step. If the elephant charged and I missed him, I should have about as much chance as a toad under a steam-roller. But even then I was not thinking particularly of my own skin, only of the watchful yellow faces behind. For at that moment, with the crowd watching me, I was not afraid in the ordinary sense, as I would have been if I had been alone. A white man mustn't be frightened in front of "natives"; and so, in general, he isn't frightened. The sole thought in my mind was that if anything went wrong those two thousand Burmans would see me pursued, caught, trampled on and reduced to a grinning corpse, like that Indian up the hill. And if that happened it was quite probable that some of them would laugh. That would never do. There was only one alternative. I shoved the cartridges into the magazine and lay down on the road to get a better aim.

The crowd grew very still, and a deep, low, happy sigh, as of people who see the theatre curtain go up at last, breathed from innumerable throats. They were going to have their bit of fun after all. The rifle was a beautiful German thing with cross-hair sights. I did not then know that in shooting an elephant one would shoot to cut an imaginary bar running from ear-hole to ear-hole. I ought, therefore, as the elephant was sideways on, to have aimed straight at his ear-hole; actually I aimed several inches in front of this, thinking the brain would be further forward.

When I pulled the trigger I did not hear the bang or feel the kick. One never does when a shot goes home—but I heard the devilish roar of glee that went up from the crowd. In that instant, in too short a time, one would have thought, even for the bullet to get there, a mysterious, terrible change had come over the elephant. He neither stirred nor fell, but every line of his body had altered. He looked suddenly stricken, shrunken, immensely old, as though the frightful impact of the bullet had paralysed him without knocking him down. At last, after what seemed a long time—it might have been five seconds, I dare say—he sagged flabbily to his knees. His mouth slobbered. An enormous senility seemed to have settled upon him. One could have imagined him thousands of years old. I fired again into the same spot. At the second shot he did not collapse but climbed with desperate slowness to his feet and stood weakly upright, with legs sagging and head drooping. I fired a third time. That was the shot that did for him. You could see the agony of it jolt his whole body and knock the last remnant of strength from his legs. But in falling he seemed for a moment to rise, for as his hind legs collapsed beneath him he seemed to tower upward like a huge rock toppling, his trunk reaching skywards like a tree. He trumpeted, for the first and only time. And then he came down, his belly towards me, with a crash that seemed to shake the ground even where I lay.

I got up. The Burmans were already racing past me across the mud. It was obvious that the elephant would never rise again, but he was not dead. He was breathing very rhythmically with long rattling gasps, his great mound of a side rising and falling. His mouth was wide open—I could see far down into the caverns of pale pink throat. I waited a long time for him to die, but his breathing did not weaken. Finally I fired my two remaining shots into the spot where I thought his heart must be. The thick blood welled out of him like red velvet, but still did not die. His body did not even jerk when the shots hit him, the tortured breathing continued without a pause. He was dying, very slowly and in great agony, but in some world remote from me where not even a bullet could damage him further. I felt that I had got to put an end to that dreadful noise. It seemed dreadful to see the great beast lying there, powerless to move and yet powerless to die, and not even to be able to finish him. I sent back for my small rifle and poured shot after shot into his heart and down his throat. They seemed to make no impression. The tortured gasps continued as steadily as the ticking of a clock.

In the end I could not stand it any longer and went away. I heard later that it took him half an hour to die. Burmans were bringing dahs and baskets even before I left, and I was told they had stripped his body almost to the bones by the afternoon.

Afterwards, of course, there were endless discussions about the shooting of the elephant. The owner was furious, but he was only an Indian and could do nothing. Besides, legally I had done the right thing, for a mad elephant has to be killed, like a mad dog, if its owner fails to control it. Among the Europeans opinion was divided. The older men said I was right, the younger men said it was a damn shame to shoot an elephant for killing a coolie, because an elephant was worth more than any damn Coringhee coolie. And afterwards I was very glad that the coolie had been killed; it put me legally in the right and it gave me a sufficient pretext for shooting the elephant. I often wondered whether any of the others grasped that I had done it solely to avoid looking a fool.

3. Self-Acceptance

Eugene C. McDanald, Jr.
Bert Kruger Smith
Robert L. Sutherland

Self-acceptance. The very word for many people conjures up a picture of peaceful and painless co-existence between man and his emotions. It implies a plateau of pleasure rather than a tedious and sometimes painful search for understanding.

Persons with professional training—psychiatrists, psychologists, social workers, and ministers have learned that true self-acceptance often comes with great difficulty or not at all. They view it as a process which involves self-awareness, self-understanding, and self-realization. They also see it as including those facets of the personality which cannot be understood but which, nevertheless, must be accepted and adjusted to on an empirical or a trial and error basis.

Three Approaches to
Self-Acceptance

Self-acceptance comes in various ways to different people. Some are able to achieve self-acceptance through their own efforts. Others need professional help. For some, the process requires a total or sub-total re-evaluation of the meaning of their emotions; others must learn to understand and accept the consequences of irrational feelings, and still others come to make an

From *Understanding Mental Health: A Common Need, A Less Frequent Achievement* by R.L. Sutherland and B.K. Smith, Van Nostrand Reinhold Company, New York, 1965. Permission granted by The Hogg Foundation for Mental Health and the authors.

empirical adjustment to inner and outer circumstances in their lives which they can neither understand nor control.

"I have been trying to accept my feeling of inferiority and unworthiness but it doesn't work. I still feel just as inferior and unworthwhile as I ever did." These were the comments of a patient after a visit to the therapist.

Learning realistic re-evaluation

This person regarded self-acceptance as a verbal process that would spirit away her unwanted feelings. However, there is a difference between being aware of feelings of inferiority and unworthiness and knowing how such emotions have come about. The patient recognized she had these emotions, but she did not understand their origin. Hence, her main need was to recognize, understand, and accept the critical experiences in her life which gave rise to her poor self-concept. To be truly self-accepting, she needed to become aware of the emotional meaning of the many significant events which had brought about her unhappy self-appraisal. If she could recall the many anxiety-laden happenings that constituted a significant portion of her life history, she might discover that the basis for her devastating self-evaluation rested on quite irrational grounds.

The story, as the patient told it, was this: Before her parents were divorced, when she was 17, neither of them had ever said anything nice to one another. They had, indeed, never said anything nice about anyone, not even her friends, whom she and others respected. A painful cluster of recollections centered on specific derogatory remarks which both parents had made about her when she did not lead her class in school. In recalling the many memories of her relationships with her parents, the patient experienced anxiety in connection with each unpleasant memory.

At first, in her therapy, she wondered what was wrong with her that she did not have a good academic standing, because she had learned prior to finishing school that she had one of the highest I.Q.'s in her class. As she progressed, her wondering about her grades was supplanted by a questioning of why her parents demanded outstanding scholastic attainment. Little by little she learned that her parents' unhappiness had something to do with the fact that they had not fulfilled the ideals they had set for themselves. She began to see that they felt inferior and unworthy in terms of their own standards.

When these realizations were reached, the patient became aware that part of her problem had stemmed from the fact that her parents had, because of their own feelings of inadequacy, wanted her to achieve goals and ideals which would provide them, through identification with her, with a sense of fulfillment. Disappointed in her, they covered her with the sense of failure and shame which had pervaded their lives.

During this tedious process of seeing how she had developed her feeling of inferiority and unworthiness, the patient learned that her parents' evluation of her was unrealistic and in marked contrast to favorable evaluations she had experienced from friends.

This insight into the real meaning of her parents' attitude came into perspective only after many hours of painful recall. Understanding the irrationality of her parents' appraisal, she re-evaluated herself and became more self-respecting.

On the negative side, then, the process of self-awareness and self-acceptance temporarily revives old anxieties; but as these problems are examined, understanding brings in its wake a reduction of anxiety. It was not easy for this patient to remind herself or share with the therapist the events in her life that made for her great inward unhappiness. She was fearful, during the months of revelation, that the therapist would react to her as if she were actually inferior and unworthy of therapeutic help.

Discomfort and realistic re-evaluation—these two processes seem to be necessary before one can gain a new appreciation of his own worth. This approach to self-acceptance involves an understanding of cause and effect. In the process of achieving a healthier self-concept, the patient in point attained insight into the causes of her illogical attitudes which made for her irrational feelings of inferiority and unworthiness.*

Understanding consequences of irrationality

In other ways, too, thoughts and feelings lying behind a pattern of behavior can be illogical. It is sometimes impossible to eliminate the irrational thoughts and feelings which give rise to a particular action because their origin is poorly understood. It is possible, however, to accept the thoughts or feelings as irrational and eliminate them as a basis for action. This is done by determining to what extent the thoughts, feelings, and action fail to conform to reality.

There is a patient who became distressed each time he discovered that his watch was missing. His first thought was, "Someone has stolen my watch." From there he would proceed to think of specific people whom he might hold suspect. As one might imagine, he always found his watch, not on or near his imagined suspects, but right where he had laid it.

On a recent occasion, when his watch was again missing, he took time to wonder about the validity of his previous suspicions; and, in a short time, he relieved himself of his habitual distress by accepting the possibility that he would probably find his watch, as he had on previous occasions, precisely where he had left it. And he did.

Now when his watch is missing, he is able to make a comfortable leap from the thought, "Someone has stolen my watch," to the immediate recognition of the possibility that he will probably find it. The leap occurs only after the development of the irrational suspicion that his watch has been stolen. But his suspicion, instead of making him uneasy, now provokes a laugh and recognition of his irrationality.**

---

*This type of self-evaluation and self-acceptance is in keeping with Freud's efforts to help patients solve problems through an understanding of the causes of their problems.

**This example supports Horney's thesis that the original cause for a course of action may not be understood, but by understanding that the motivating thought-feeling and the ensuing action have no basis in reality, the action itself and its consequences may be modified.

Making Empirical Adjustment

Both of the aforementioned approaches to self-acceptance are useful in relieving many anxieties, but the fact must also be accepted that one cannot solve all problems or difficulties by either process. When neither of these approaches leads to the lessening of a problem, then the only helpful alternative is to accept and remain aware of the problem with the hope that a practical adjustment to it may be worked out now and that an understanding of it may possibly be achieved later.

For example, a person may be a victim of stage-fright in public speaking. Though he does not understand the basis for his distress, he may realize that the cause of his present anxiety is irrational. Understanding that his anxiety is unreasonable may not help; yet he may adjust to his discomfort, as many people do, by enduring it. Or, he may adjust by refusing to make speeches. He may, however, in the course of time, eliminate some of the anxiety of public speaking by acquiring confidence through continuing to make public appearances. Regardless of the adjustment he makes to stage-fright, he must accept the present adjustment as perhaps the best that he can make at the moment and hope that at a later date he will be able to understand its cause.***

Here the question may be raised as to how the first two modes of self-acceptance differ from the third type which involves an empirical positive or negative adjustment to a problem that does not at the moment lend itself to any form of logical resolution.

The first two methods of self-acceptance are dynamic: they clarify and make for growth. On the other hand, adjustment *per se,* or empirical adjustment, is more or less static; that is, it keeps matters from getting better or worse. Yet, the several modes of self-acceptance, though different, are interrelated. They are allied because they complement one another in contributing to the maintenance of mental and emotional balance. They are also interrelated in the sense

***Adolph Meyer urged his patients to make the best possible empirical adjustment to problems that did not lend themselves to logical resolution. One of the questions which he routinely asked patients was, "If your best friend had your problem, what would you advise him to do about it?"

that a problem one simply adjusts to today may later be understood and thereby contribute to one's growth and creativity.

Self-acceptance, then, occurs at three levels. On one level it includes an awareness, understanding, and acceptance of the causes of one's problems. At another level, when the cause cannot be understood, it involves an acceptance of one's irrational psychic processes and a realistic evaluation of the behavior which these irrational processes produce. At still another level, it involves an acceptance of problems which cannot be in any sense understood rationally but which may be adjusted to on an intuitive or a trial and error basis.

The Self-Accepting Process

One hears frequently of certain individuals who are described as "well-adjusted," and it might be appropriate to consider how reality-oriented and self-accepting these people are.

Examples

Some of these so-called "well-adjusted" people give evidence of solid emotional health because they are self-accepting, life-accepting, and capable of reckoning with current realities.

The "pseudo" well-adjusted person. Others, however, give the appearance of health because they use a fairly reliable set of blind spots for handling or ignoring all kinds of life situations. They conceal their difficulties in living so well that they appear to be problem-free. Yet, the rut they are in precludes the possibility of self-awareness and personal growth.

These people, in their fixed responses to life, perceive new experiences somewhat like the observer in the peep-hole experiment. The experiment goes this way: Three peep-holes are arranged in order. Behind the first peep-hole are four wires of equal length forming a square. Behind the second peep-hole are four wires of equal length forming a parallelogram. Behind the third peep-hole are four wires of equal length placed at random. If one looks through the first peep-hole, he sees a square. If, immediately thereafter, he looks through the second and third peep-holes in rapid succession, he still sees squares. In short, new experiences in the form of rearrangements of wires of equal length are provided; yet, the uniqueness of each pattern is lost because the initial peep-hole experience distorts each succeeding new arrangement of wires and causes them to be seen in terms of the first experience.

The failure to perceive "what is" may not be important if it is only a matter of misperception of the arrangement of four wires. If, however, misperceptions occur in a person's reactions to life situations, they may lead to serious errors in judgment and behavior. For example, the optimist who experiences life predominantly through the positive after-image of favorable early life experiences may disregard certain unfavorable developments in his current life situation. Conversely, the pessimist who experiences life largely through the negative after-image of unfavorable early life experiences, may fail to perceive the favorable factors in present occurrences, with the result that he despairs unrealistically.

A pessimist. For example, an attractive red-headed girl just a little past her teens, felt that, "Life will never offer me any happiness." She had these feelings despite the fact that she was holding a good job.

Once she remarked that when she did have an optimistic feeling, she immediately thrust it aside because it was too painful for her to be tantalized by the possibility that her life could be different. The therapist dared her to hold on to this optimistic feeling when it next occurred and to see what thoughts, feelings, and memories might come along with it.

Some time after this suggestion was made, she said she was about to go to her beauty parlor appointment, when again she experienced a mild glow of optimism. She held on to this feeling, and while at the beauty parlor, it occurred to her for several months there had been in her life favorable developments of which she had taken only passing notice. In reviewing them, she realized that the people in her office were treating her with respect and not pushing her around, as she had anticipated they would do after the newness of her relation to them wore off. She realized, too, that her parents no longer came to town unannounced to check on her, as they had done when she was in college. What surprised her most was that during her parents' last visit, when she informed them that she had a date, they left her apartment before her friend arrived, in contrast to their previous habit of meeting and approving, or disapproving, of each boy who took her out.

This girl's acceptance of her optimism resulted in her making a significant communication to herself, namely, that life, contrary to her previous feeling that it could not be different, actually was already different. She did not, however, become aware of this fact until she permitted the optimistic feeling to speak its message.

Clinically, it is well known that each feeling contains a special revelation, which one can frequently apprehend by holding onto and remaining aware of the story that unfolds in connection with it. Not all revelations are as pleasant, however, as the case of the pessimistic girl. Some are quite painful. This is especially so with the type of person who is unaware of the fact that he is highly self-righteous. Such a person suffers from a form of blindness in which the self-revealing and self-accepting process is especially resisted.

A self-righteous man. The second patient may illustrate such a person. This man in his early thirties, slim-built, muscular, self-righteous, had been in therapy for many months. He seldom relaxed but seemed to hold both his body and his emotions taut. On this particular day, he spoke of the sadistic qualities he saw in his fiancee. The therapist listened to him for a while. Then, because he had learned to know the man during the weeks he had been in therapy, he commented that perhaps the qualities he saw in his fiancee might be a reflection of his own sadistic behavior toward her.

Within a moment, the patient changed into a man of violence. He spoke words of abuse to the therapist. He rose to leave, his eyes staring with anger. The therapist held on to his poise and pursued the point by saying, "I'm sorry you don't have the courage to stick around and listen to the facts."

It took a bit of time for the words to hit home. When they did, the man paused, returned to his chair, and sat down. The doctor then went into his charges against his fiancee, pointing up that the unsportsmanlike manipulations of which he accused his fiancee were the self-same manipulations which characterized his behavior in relationship to her and the therapist.

After a lengthy protest that he was not capable of such behavior, he suddenly stood up; and while pounding the wall with his fist, said, "Well, maybe I have been damnably inconsiderate and demanding. What do I do about it?" This statement was the beginning of a painful awareness of sadistic tendencies within himself, and his sadism, which previously was outwardly directed, now became directed toward himself in the form of guilt, depression, and self-depreciation.

Months elapsed from that afternoon until his depression lightened, months before he could begin to understand his tendencies. One day he came into the office, eager to talk, words tumbling over one another. "Doctor," he said excitedly, "I had a dream last night. There was a little boy in knee pants and white shirt standing on a dirt street. All of a sudden a runaway horse appeared at the corner and came rushing toward the little boy, who was rooted with fright. Then, even as the flying dirt from the horse's hooves blinded him, a grandmotherly woman ran into the street and snatched him up."

When the therapist asked him how he interpreted the dream, he replied, "In thinking about this dream, I felt quite keenly that I have been running over people with my harsh, judgmental attitudes more or less like the runaway horse that almost ran over the little boy."

"And who was the little boy?"

At first he replied, "Why, I just told you. He stands for the other people that I have been trampling all my life."

The doctor prodded him a bit by saying, "Have you forgotten the little boy you carry within yourself, a youngster who would like a little grandmotherly loving from none other than you?"

The man's lips began to tremble. He turned his head away to hide the tears, but in a moment he was weeping like a child. He cried because he wanted to be tender and understanding with the immature aspects of himself, rather than harsh and judgmental, as his parents had been toward him when he was little. This was a critical point in his achievement of self-acceptance, which came hard and after a bitter battle within himself.

Methods of Achieving Self-Acceptance

When people see how self-acceptance helps clear away the brush of unneeded anxiety, they are likely to generalize by asking if self-acceptance can be achieved through a do-it-yourself approach or if professional help is always needed. Can a person learn to see through his own irrational behavior?

The answer is that some people can work through their problems in their own fashion, while others need the help of a therapist.

One person who appeared to need the counsel of a psychiatrist was a slim brunette in her mid-thirties. Her chic clothes and smart coiffure made her look like a busy clubwoman, satisfied with her way of life. Instead, when she came to the therapist, she had already spent years in loathing herself for extramarital affairs which she claimed she could not avoid. She said, "When I make up my mind to get out of one mess, I get into another."

She told the lurid details of her out-of-wedlock sex life. The interesting aspect of it was that sex gave her no basic emotional satisfaction despite the fact that there was nothing pleasurable missing in the physical aspects of her sex life. She doubted not her sexual competence, but her ability to secure love and to be loved. To erase the doubt, she vainly attempted to use sex as a medium of securing acceptance. Yet that did not work. The affairs only created self-loathing and deepened her doubts about being a lovable person.

One day when she came to her therapy hour, she was quite despondent. Her hands lay motionless on her lap. In a quiet voice she said that she knew she had ruined her life and was only a source of anxiety to her husband

and family. Then she looked straight ahead and said, "But now I have found a way to relieve my family of further anxiety. I am going to commit suicide."

Instead of attempting to dissuade her, the therapist answered with great exasperation. "The only decent thing you can do is understand this messed-up life of yours and do something about it."

The patient responded with shock, with hurt, and total surprise. But she continued to talk, only with more emphasis on her feelings and less on her actions. It took many weeks before she began to understand herself and before she could say to the therapist, "When I look back now and try to see what started me on the road to finding myself, it seems that it all began the day you got mad at me for saying suicide was the best thing for all concerned."

As she spoke, the doctor was aware that the patient was developing insights into herself and her relationships with other people, insights which some people might have been able to attain through painful self-study but for which she needed the aid of a psychiatrist. In that foregone critical hour she had accepted the therapist's anger at her suicidal idea as evidence that she could be worthwhile in her own estimation if she would only dare to accept her messed-up self and proceed to understand it.

When this patient had achieved a fair understanding of herself, she returned home, and after being there for awhile, wrote the doctor a letter, some of which read as follows: "I think we did a pretty good job on me, but since I've been home, I discovered that a girl who had problems similar to mine had somehow worked things out pretty well by herself. When I talked to her about what you and I did, I found that she had arrived at some of the same answers that we did. Although I'm a little envious, I tell myself that I'm really not inferior to her, and that I just needed more help than she."

The story of this woman's difficulties, and the excerpt from her letter, highlight two things. The first is that, regardless of what it is a person does not like about himself, the kindest thing he can do in his own behalf is to accept and try to understand it, rather than sit in

perpetual self-devastating judgment on himself as a bad
or an unlikable person. The second is that a person can
work out a good many things unaided. It took a great
deal of courage for the patient's friend to "keep
appointments" with herself and to be self-accepting and
understanding in the ongoing sense of these terms.

The self-accepting process, then, is one through which
persons are able to achieve a measure of understanding
about themselves and then are able to handle problems
more adequately. When this process becomes an integral
part of one's life, the result is a self-accepting man or
woman.

The Self-Accepting Person

The fully accepting person, then, is one who can
become acquainted with the positive and negative ways
he views life in order to be able to make a reasonably
accurate evaluation of realities in everyday living.

Exemplified by Goethe

The German poet, Goethe, may well serve as a good
example of a fully self-accepting person. "I have never
heard of any crime which I might not have committed."
These are the words he is quoted as having said! They
may startle one by the frank admission of criminal
thoughts and feelings; one may well wonder how
Goethe, a person whose life was rich in creative
fulfillment, could be at the same time Goethe, the
person who had never heard of a crime he might not
have committed. However, one can progress from seeing
the two as incompatible to seeing them as being part
and parcel of life, Goethe's life, and *every* man's.

There is no person in history, past or present, who
has not experienced the wish to love and the wish to
destroy. The ultimately important idea is not whether
these thoughts and feelings are regarded as good or bad,
but how they are handled. If one focuses for a moment
on what to do with a destructive impulse, murder, for
instance, he might recall what Christ is reported to have
said in the fifth chapter of St. Matthew's gospel, "But I
say unto you that ye resist not evil." This rather

startling statement may be misinterpreted. Some might say if, then, one has a murderous desire, would the import of Chirst's teaching be that he not resist being fully aware of the desire? The answer to that is an unequivocal "yes." Modern psychology is in agreement with Christ's teaching about the handling of a destructive impulse and says, "Don't resist being aware of a murderous desire; realize that it is a part of you; instead of hating the fact that you have such a feeling, accept and understand it. If you accept and understand it, you will have no overwhelming tendency to commit criminal acts. You can then handle your left-over aggressive feelings in ways that are fun, as through vigorous sports or identification with a mystery book murderer."

Goethe accepted his criminal tendencies, and thereby enriched his creativity. One may infer that he did not push his destructive ideas aside nor deny them; rather, he kept them on a level of awareness and under control. In so doing, he did not run the risk of their building up unconsciously to an intensity where they would, in effect, make his body their instrument.

Goethe's self-acceptance made for health and creativity, and modern dynamic psychiatry and psychology support Goethe's approach to life as a valid one. What, then, can be said about the characteristics of the self-accepting person? Are there some "rules of thumb" by which we recognize him?

Some Characteristics

The self-accepting person is a participant in life rather than a spectator.

He is inclined to be objective, spontaneous, and emotionally and intellectually honest.

He tries to understand the interpersonal and environmental problems he faces, but he also accepts his limitations in gaining true insight concerning them.

He works out the best adjustment to life of which he is capable, often without fully understanding all that is involved.

However, he is willing to experience the pleasures and discomforts of self-revelation: i.e., he accepts the mixed pain and joy that accompany each change in his attitude and feeling toward himself and others.

His claims on life are, for the most part, reasonable. If he wants to be a member of the Country Club and yet cannot afford it, he finds other social and recreational outlets in keeping with his budget.

The self-accepting person without special talent or ability is able to share emotionally in the gifts of others without undue regret about his inborn deficiencies.

He does not brood about missed opportunities, lost causes, errors, and failures. Rather, he looks on them for what they can contribute to his doing things differently or better in the future.

He does not get stuck in the rut of irrational feelings of love, hate, envy, jealousy, suspicion, lust, and greed, because he lets each feeling spell out its special message for him.

Although the self-accepting person may prefer not to be alone or isolated from family or friends, yet, in special times, when aloneness or isolation is a necessity, he can endure lack of contact with his fellows.

The self-accepting person may or may not be conventional in his thinking, feeling, or behavior. But when he is unconventional, it is not for the purpose of flaunting convention but rather for the sake of expressing or fulfilling a valid personal or public need.

He is not rigidly guided by rules and moralisms; hence he is willing to alter values in keeping with new insights.

He grants to others their right to values not identical with his own.

The self-accepting person puts himself into life in terms of his highest insights. Yet he accepts the fact that, in its essence, it remains the mystery of mysteries.

. . .

Self-acceptance, then, in the ongoing sense of the term is a task demanding maturity. The rewards of this process are manifold—the adjustment to or reduction of personal difficulties in living and a greater realization of one's potential as a person. With this realization, one can reach out to become a reasonably productive member of the larger world of which he is a part.

4. Some Hypotheses Regarding the Facilitation of Personal Growth

Carl R. Rogers

To be faced by a troubled, conflicted person who is seeking and expecting help, has already constituted a great challenge to me. Do I have the knowledge, the resources, the psychological strength, the skill—do I have whatever it takes to be of help to such an individual?

For more than twenty-five years I have been trying to meet this kind of challenge. It has caused me to draw upon every element of my professional background: the rigorous methods of personality measurement which I first learned at Teachers' College, Columbia; the Freudian psychoanalytic insights and methods of the Institute for Child Guidance where I worked as interne; the continuing developments in the field of clinical psychology, with which I have been closely associated; the briefer exposure to the work of Otto Rank, to the methods of psychiatric social work, and other resources too numerous to mention. But most of all it has meant a continual learning from my own experience and that of my colleagues at the Counseling Center as we have endeavored to discover for ourselves effective means of working with people in distress. Gradually I have developed a way of working which grows out of that experience, and which can be tested, refined, and reshaped by further experience and by research.

A General Hypothesis

One brief way of describing the change which has taken place in me is to say that in my early professional years I was asking the question, How can I treat, or cure, or change this person? Now I would phrase the question in this way: How can I provide a relationship which this person may use for his own personal growth?

It is as I have come to put the question in this second way that I realize that whatever I have learned is applicable to all of my human relationships, not just to working with clients with problems. It is for this reason that I feel it is possible that the learnings which have had meaning for me in my experience may have some meaning for you in your experience, since all of us are involved in human relationships.

Perhaps I should start with a negative learning. It has gradually been driven home to me that I cannot be of help to this troubled person by means of any intellectual or training procedure. No approach which relies upon knowledge, upon training, upon the acceptance of something that is *taught,* is of any use. These approaches seem so tempting and direct that I have, in the past, tried a great many of them. It is possible to explain a person to himself, to prescribe steps which should lead him forward, to train him in knowledge about a more satisfying mode of life. But such methods are, in my experience, futile and inconsequential. The most they can accomplish is some temporary change, which soon disappears, leaving the individual more than ever convinced of his inadequacy.

The failure of any such approach through the intellect has forced me to recognize that change appears to come about through experience in a relationship. So I am going to try to state very briefly and informally, some of the essential hypotheses regarding a helping relationship which have seemed to gain increasing confirmation both from experience and research.

I can state the over-all hypothesis in one sentence, as follows. If I can provide a certain type of relationship, the other person will discover within himself the capacity to use that relationship for growth, and change and personal development will occur.

The Relationship

But what meaning do these terms have? Let me take separately the three major phrases in this sentence and indicate something of the meaning they have for me. What is this certain type of relationship I would like to provide?

I have found that the more that I can be genuine in the relationship, the more helpful it will be. This means that I need to be aware of my own feelings, in so far as possible, rather than presenting an outward façade of one attitude, while actually holding another attitude at a deeper or unconscious level. Being genuine also involves the willingness to be and to express, in my words and my behavior, the various feelings and attitudes which exist in me. It is only in this way that the relationship can have *reality,* and reality seems deeply important as a first condition. It is only by providing the genuine reality which is in me, that the other person can successfully seek for the reality in him. I have found this to be true even when the attitudes I feel are not attitudes with which I am pleased, or attitudes which seem conducive to a good relationship. It seems extremely important to be *real.*

As a second condition, I find that the more acceptance and liking I feel toward this individual, the more I will be creating a relationship which he can use. By acceptance I mean a warm regard for him as a person of unconditional self-worth—of value no matter what his condition, his behavior, or his feelings. It means a respect and liking for him as a separate person, a willingness for him to possess his own feelings in his own way. It means an acceptance of and regard for his attitudes of the moment, no matter how negative or positive, no matter how much they may contradict other attitudes he has held in the past. This acceptance of each fluctuating aspect of this other person makes it for him a relationship of warmth and safety, and the safety of being liked and prized as a person seems a highly important element in a helping relationship.

I also find that the relationship is significant to the extent the I feel a continuing desire to understand—a sensitive empathy with each of the client's feelings and communications as they seem to him at that moment. Acceptance does not mean much until it involves understanding. It is only as I *understand* the feelings and thoughts which seem so horrible to you, or so weak, or so sentimental, or so bizarre—it is only as I see them as you see them, and accept them and you, that you feel really free to explore all the hidden nooks and frightening crannies of your inner and often buried experience. This *freedom* is an important condition of the relationship. There is implied here a freedom to explore oneself at both conscious and unconscious levels, as rapidly as one can dare to embark on this dangerous quest. There is also a complete freedom from any type of moral or diagnostic evaluation, since all such evaluations are, I believe, always threatening.

Thus the relationship which I have found helpful is characterized by a sort of transparency on my part, in which my real feelings are evident; by an acceptance of this other person as a separate person with value in his own right; and by a deep empathic understanding which enables me to see his private world through his eyes. When these conditions are achieved, I become a companion to my client, accompanying him in the frightening search for himself, which he now feels free to undertake.

I am by no means always able to achieve this kind of relationship with another, and sometimes, even when I feel I have achieved it in myself, he may be too frightened to perceive what is being offered to him. But I would say that when I hold in myself the kind of attitudes I have described, and when the other person can to some degree experience these attitudes, then I believe that change and constructive personal development will *invariably* occur—and I include the word "invariably" only after long and careful consideration.

The Motivation for Change

So much for the relationship. The second phrase in my overall hypothesis was that the individual will discover within himself the capacity to use this relationship for growth. I will try to indicate something of the meaning which that phrase has for me. Gradually my experience has forced me to conclude that the individual has within himself the capacity and the tendency, latent if not evident, to move forward toward maturity. In a suitable psychological climate this tendency is released, and becomes actual rather than potential. It is evident in the capacity of the individual to understand those aspects of his life and of himself which are causing him pain and dissatisfaction, an understanding which probes beneath his conscious knowledge of himself into those experiences which he has hidden from himself because of their threatening nature. It shows itself in the tendency to reorganize his personality and his relationship to life in ways which are regarded as more mature. Whether one calls it a growth tendency, a drive toward self-actualization, or a forward-moving directional tendency, it is the mainspring of life, and is, in the last analysis, the tendency upon which all psychotherapy depends. It is the urge which is evident in all organic and human life—to expand, extend, become autonomous, develop, mature—the tendency to express and activate all the capacities of the organism, to the extent that such activation enhances the organism or the self. This tendency may become deeply buried under layer after layer of encrusted psychological defenses; it may be hidden behind elaborate facades which deny its existence; but it is my belief that it exists in every individual, and awaits only the proper conditions to be released and expressed.

The Outcomes

I have attempted to describe the relationship which is basic to constructive personality change. I have tried to put into words the type of capacity which the individual brings to such a relationship. The third phrase of my general statement was that change and personal development would occur. It is my hypothesis that in such a relationship the individual will reorganize himself at both the conscious and deeper levels of his personality in such a manner as to cope with life more constructively, more intelligently, and in a more socialized as well as a more satisfying way.

Here I can depart from speculation and bring in the steadily increasing body of solid research knowledge which is accumulating. We know now that individuals who live in such a relationship even for a relatively limited number of hours show profound and significant changes in personality, attitudes, and behavior, changes that do not occur in matched control groups. In such a relationship the individual becomes more integrated, more effective. He shows fewer of the characteristics which are usually termed neurotic or psychotic, and more of the characteristics of the healthy, well-functioning person. He changes his perception of himself, becoming more realistic in his views of self. He becomes more like the person he wishes to be. He values himself more highly. He is more self-confident and self-directing. He has a better understanding of himself, becomes more open to his experience, denies or represses less of his experience. He becomes more accepting in his attitudes toward others, seeing others as more similar to himself.

In his behavior he shows similar changes. He is less frustrated by stress, and recovers from stress more quickly. He becomes more mature in his everyday behavior as this is observed by friends. He is less defensive, more adaptive, more able to meet situations creatively.

These are some of the changes which we now know come about in individuals who have completed a series of counseling interviews in which the psychological atmosphere approximates the relationship I described. Each of the statements made is based upon objective evidence. Much more research needs to be done, but there can no longer be any doubt as to the effectiveness of such a relationship in producing personality change.

A Broad Hypothesis of Human Relationships

To me, the exciting thing about these research findings is not simply the fact that they give evidence of the efficacy of one form of psychotherapy, though that is by no means unimportant. The excitement comes from the fact that these findings justify an even broader hypothesis regarding all human relationships. There seems every reason to suppose that the therapeutic relationship is only one instance of interpersonal relations, and that the same lawfulness governs all such relationships. Thus it seems reasonable to hypothesize that if the parent creates with his child a psychological climate, such as we have described, then the child will become more self-directing, socialized, and mature. To the extent that the teacher creates such a relationship with his class, the student will become a self-initiated learner, more original, more self-disciplined, less anxious and other-directed. If the administrator, or military or industrial leader, creates such a climate within his organization, then his staff will become more self-responsible, more creative, better able to adapt to new problems, more basically cooperative. It appears possible to me that we are seeing the emergence of a new field of human relationships, in which we may specify that if certain attitudinal conditions exist, then certain definable changes will occur.

Conclusion

Let me conclude by returning to a personal statement. I have tried to share with you something of what I have learned in trying to be of help to troubled, unhappy, maladjusted individuals. I have formulated the hypothesis which has gradually come to have meaning for me—not only in my relationship to clients in distress, but in all my human relationships. I have indicated that such research knowledge as we have supports this hypothesis, but that there is much more investigation needed. I should like now to pull together into one statement the conditions of this general hypothesis, and the effects which are specified.

If I can create a relationship characterized on my part:

- by a genuineness and transparency, in which I am my real feelings;
- by a warm acceptance of and prizing of the other person as a separate individual;
- by a sensitive ability to see his world and himself as he sees them;

Then the other individual in the relationship:
  will experience and understand aspects of himself
      which previously he has repressed;
  will find himself becoming better integrated, more
      able to function effectively;
  will become more similar to the person he would
      like to be;
  will be more self-directing and self-confident;
  will become more of a person, more unique and
      more self-expressive;
  will be more understanding, more acceptant of
      others;
  will be able to cope with the problems of life more
      adequately and more comfortably.

I believe that this statement holds whether I am speaking of my relationship with a client, with a group of students or staff members, with my family or children. It seems to me that we have here a general hypothesis which offers exciting possibilities for the development of creative, adaptive, autonomous persons.

5. What It Means to Become a Person

Carl R. Rogers

In my work at the Counseling Center of the University of Chicago, I have the opportunity of working with people who present a wide variety of personal problems. There is the student concerned about failing in college; the housewife disturbed about her marriage; the individual who feels he is teetering on the edge of a complete breakdown or psychosis; the responsible professional man who spends much of his time in sexual fantasies and functions inefficiently in his work; the brilliant student, at the top of his class, who is paralyzed by the conviction that he is hopelessly and helplessly inadequate; the parent who is distressed by his child's behavior; the popular girl who finds herself unaccountably overtaken by sharp spells of black depression; the woman who fears that life and love are passing her by, and that her good graduate record is a poor recompense; the man who has become convinced that powerful or sinister forces are plotting against him;—I could go on and on with the many different and unique problems which people bring to us. They run the gamut of life's experiences. Yet there is no satisfaction in giving this type of catalog, for, as counselor, I know that the problem as stated in the first interview will not be the problem as seen in the second or third hour, and by the tenth interview it will be a still different problem or series of problems.

From *On Becoming a Person* by Carl R. Rogers, Houghton Mifflin Company, 1961. Copyright © 1961 by Carl R. Rogers. Permission granted by Houghton Mifflin Company and Carl R. Rogers.

I have however come to believe that in spite of this bewildering horizontal multiplicity, and the layer upon layer of vertical complexity, there is perhaps only one problem. As I follow the experience of many clients in the therapeutic relationship which we endeavor to create for them, it seems to me that each one is raising the same question. Below the level of the problem situation about which the individual is complaining—behind the trouble with studies, or wife, or employer, or with his own uncontrollable or bizarre behavior, or with his frightening feelings, lies one central search. It seems to me that at bottom each person is asking, "Who am I, *really*? How can I get in touch with this real self, underlying all my surface behavior? How can I become myself?"

The Process of Becoming

Getting Behind the Mask

Let me try to explain what I mean when I say that it appears that the goal the individual most wishes to achieve, the end which he knowingly and unknowingly pursues, is to become himself.

When a person comes to me, troubled by his unique combination of difficulties, I have found it most worth while to try to create a relationship with him in which he is safe and free. It is my purpose to understand the way he feels in his own world, to accept him as he is, to create an atmosphere of freedom in which he can move in his thinking and feeling and being, in any direction he desires. How does he use this freedom?

It is my experience that he uses it to become more and more himself. He begins to drop the false fronts, or the masks, or the roles, with which he has faced life. He appears to be trying to discover something more basic, something more truly himself. At first he lays aside masks which he is to some degree aware of using. One young woman student describes in a counseling interview one of the masks she has been using, and how uncertain she is whether underneath this appeasing, ingratiating front there is any real self with convictions.

> I was thinking about this business of standards. I somehow developed a sort of knack, I guess, of—well—habit—of trying to make people feel at ease around me, or to make things go along smoothly. There always had to be some appeaser around, being sorta the oil that soothed the waters. At a small meeting, or a little party, or something—I could help things go along nicely and appear to be having a good time. And sometimes I'd surprise myself by arguing against what I really thought when I saw that the person in charge would be quite unhappy about it if I didn't. In other words I just wasn't ever—I mean, I didn't find myself ever being set and definite about things. Now the reason why I did it probably was I'd been doing it around home so much. I just didn't stand up for my own convictions, until I don't know whether I have any convictions to stand up for. I haven't been really honestly being myself, or actually knowing what my real self is, and I've been just playing a sort of false role.

You can, in this excerpt, see her examining the mask she has been using, recognizing her dissatisfaction with it, and wondering how to get to the real self underneath, if such a self exists.

In this attempt to discover his own self, the client typically uses the relationship to explore, to examine the various aspects of his own experience, to recognize and face up to the deep contradictions which he often discovers. He learns how much of his behavior, even how much of the feeling he experiences, is not real, is not something which flows from the genuine reactions of his organism, but is a façade, a front, behind which he has been hiding. He discovers how much of his life is guided by what he thinks he *should* be, not by what he is. Often he discovers that he exists only in response to the demands of others, that he seems to have no self of his own, that he is only trying to think, and feel, and behave in the way that others believe he *ought* to think, and feel and behave.

In this connection I have been astonished to find how accurately the Danish philosopher, Søren Kierkegaard, pictured the dilemma of the individual more than a century ago, with keen psychological insight. He points out that the most common despair is to be in despair at not choosing, or willing, to be onself; but that the deepest form of despair is to choose "to be another than himself." On the other hand "to will to be that self which one truly is, is indeed the opposite of despair," and this choice is the deepest responsibility of man. As I read some of his writings I almost feel that he must have listened in on the statements made by our clients as they search and explore for the reality of self—often a painful and troubling search.

This exploration becomes even more disturbing when they find themselves involved in removing the false faces which they had not known were false faces. They begin to engage in the frightening task of exploring the turbulent and sometimes violent feelings within themselves. To remove a mask which you had thought was part of your self can be a deeply disturbing experience, yet when there is freedom to think and feel and be, the individual moves toward such a goal. A few statements from a person who had completed a series of psychotherapeutic interviews, will illustrate this. She uses many metaphors as she tells how she struggled to get to the core of herself.

> As I look at it now, I was peeling off layer after layer of defenses. I'd build them up, try them, and then discard them when you remained the same. I didn't know what was at the bottom and I was very much afraid to find out, but I *had* to keep on trying. At first I felt there was nothing within me—just a great emptiness where I needed and wanted a solid core. Then I began to feel that I was facing a solid brick wall, too high to get over and too thick to go through. One day the wall became translucent, rather than solid. After this, the wall seemed to disappear but beyond it I discovered a dam holding back violent, churning waters. I felt as if I were holding back the force of these waters and if I opened even a tiny hole I and all about me would be destroyed in the ensuing torrent of feelings represented by the water. Finally I could stand the strain no longer and I let go. All I did, actually, was to succumb to complete and utter self pity, then hate, then love. After this experience, I felt as if I had leaped a brink and was safely on the other side, though still tottering a bit on the edge. I don't know what I was searching for or where I was going, but I felt then as I have always felt whenever I really lived, that I was moving forward.

I believe this represents rather well the feelings of many an individual that if the false front, the wall, the dam, is not maintained, then everything will be swept away in the violence of the feelings that he discovers pent-up in his private world. Yet it also illustrates the compelling necessity which the individual feels to search for and become himself. It also begins to indicate the way in which the individual determines the reality in himself—that when he fully experiences the feelings which at an organic level he *is,* as this client experienced her self-pity, hatred, and love, then he feels an assurance that he is being a part of his real self.

The Experiencing of Feeling

I would like to say something more about this experiencing of feeling. It is really the discovery of unknown elements of self. The phenomenon I am trying to describe is something which I think is quite difficult to get across in any meaningful way. In our daily lives there are a thousand and one reasons for not letting ourselves experience our attitudes fully, reasons from our past and from the present, reasons that reside within the social situation. It seems too dangerous, too potentially damaging, to experience them freely and fully. But in the safety and freedom of the therapeutic relationship, they can be experienced fully, clear to the limit of what they are. They can be and are experienced in a fashion that I like to think of as a "pure culture," so that for the moment the person *is* his fear, or he *is* his anger, or he *is* his tenderness, or whatever.

Perhaps again I can clarify this by giving an example from a client which will indicate and convey something of what I mean. A young man, a graduate student who is deep in therapy, has been puzzling over a vague feeling which he senses in himself. He gradually identifies it as a frightened feeling of some kind, a fear of failing, a fear of not getting his Ph.D. Then comes a long pause. From this point on we will let the recorded interview speak for itself.

> *Client:* I was kinda letting it seep through. But I also tied it in with you and with my relationship with you. And that's one thing I feel about it is kind of a fear of it going away; or that's another thing—it's so hard to get hold of—there's kind of two pulling feelings about it. Or two "me's" somehow. One is the scared one that wants to hold on to things, and that one I guess I can feel pretty clearly right now. You know, I kinda need things to hold on to—and I feel kinda scared.

Therapist: M-hm. That's something you can feel right this minute, and have been feeling and perhaps *are* feeling in regard to our relationship, too.

C: Won't you let me *have* this, because, you know, I kinda *need* it. I can be so lonely and scared without it.

T: M-hm, m-hm. Let me hang on to this because I'd be terribly scared if I didn't. Let me *hold* on to it. (*Pause*)

C: It's kinda the same thing—*Won't* you let me have my thesis or my Ph.D. so then . . . 'Cause I kinda *need* that little world. I mean. . . .

T: In both instances it's kind of a pleading thing too, isn't it? Let me *have* this because I need it *badly.* I'd be awfully frightened without it. (*Long pause.*)

C: I get a sense of . . . I can't somehow get much further . . . It's this kind of *pleading* little boy, somehow, even . . . What's this gesture of begging? (*Putting his hands together as if in prayer*) Isn't it funny? 'Cause that . . .

T: You put your hands in sort of a supplication.

C: Ya, that's right! Won't you *do* this for me, kinda . . . Oh, that's *terrible!* Who, me, *beg*?

Perhaps this excerpt will convey a bit of the thing I have been talking about, the experiencing of a feeling all the way to the limit. Here he is, for a moment, experiencing himself as nothing but a pleading little boy, supplicating, begging, dependent. At that moment he is nothing but his pleadingness, all the way through. To be sure he almost immediately backs away from this experiencing by saying "Who, me, *beg*?" but it has left its mark. As he says a moment later, "It's such a wondrous thing to have these new things come out of me. It amazes me so much each time, and then again there's that same feeling, kind of feeling scared that I've so much of this that I'm keeping back or something." He realizes that this has bubbled through, and that for the moment he *is* his dependency, in a way which astonishes him.

It is not only dependency that is experienced in this all-out kind of fashion. It may be hurt, or sorrow, or jealousy, or destructive anger, or deep desire, or confidence and pride, or sensitive tenderness, or out-going love. It may be any of the emotions of which man is capable.

What I have gradually learned from experiences such as this, is that the individual in such a moment, is coming to *be* what he *is*. When a person has, throughout therapy, experienced in this fashion all the emotions which organismically arise in him, and has experienced them in this knowing and open manner, then he has experienced *himself,* in all the richness that exists within himself. He has become what he is.

The Discovery of Self in Experience

Let us pursue a bit further this question of what it means to become one's self. It is a most perplexing question and again I will try to take from a statement by a client, written between interviews, a suggestion of an answer. She tells how the various façades by which she has been living have somehow crumpled and collapsed, bringing a feeling of confusion, but also a feeling of relief. She continues:

> You know, it seems as if all the energy that went into holding the arbitrary pattern together was quite unnecessary—a waste. You think you have to make the pattern yourself; but there are so many pieces, and it's so hard to see where they fit. Sometimes you put them in the wrong place, and the more pieces mis-fitted, the more effort it takes to hold them in place, until at last you are so tired that even that awful confusion is better than holding on any longer. Then you discover that left to themselves the jumbled pieces fall quite naturally into their own places, and a living pattern emerges without any effort at all on your part. Your job is just to discover it, and in the course of that, you will find yourself and your own place. You must even let your own experience tell you its own meaning; the minute *you* tell it what it means, you are at war with yourself.

Let me see if I can take her poetic expression and translate it into the meaning it has for me. I believe she is saying that to be herself means to find the pattern, the underlying order, which exists in the ceaselessly changing flow of her experience. Rather than to try to hold her experience into the form of a mask; or to make it be a form or structure that it is not, being herself means to discover the unity and harmony which exists in her own actual feelings and reactions. It means that the real self is something which is comfortably dis-covered in one's experiences, not something imposed upon it.

Through giving excerpts from the statements of these clients, I have been trying to suggest what happens in the warmth and understanding of a facilitating relationship with a therapist. It seems that gradually, painfully, the individual explores what is behind the masks he presents to the world, and even behind the masks with which he has been deceiving himself. Deeply and often vividly he experiences the various elements of himself which have been hidden within. Thus to an increasing degree he becomes himself—not a façade of conformity to others, not a cynical denial of all feeling, nor a front of intellectual rationality, but a living, breathing, feeling, fluctuating process—in short, he becomes a person.

The Person Who Emerges

I imagine that some of you are asking, "But what *kind* of a person does he become? It isn't enough to say that he drops the façades. What kind of person lies underneath?" Since one of the most obvious facts is that each individual tends to become a separate and distinct and unique person, the answer is not easy. However I would like to point out some of the characteristic trends which I see. No one person would fully exemplify these characteristics, no one person fully achieves the description I will give, but I do see certain generalizations which can be drawn, based upon living a therapeutic relationship with many clients.

Openness to Experience

First of all I would say that in this process the individual becomes more open to his experience. This is a phrase which has come to have a great deal of meaning to me. It is the opposite of defensiveness. Psychological research has shown that if the evidence of our senses runs contrary to our picture of self, then that evidence is distorted. In other words we cannot see all that our senses report, but only the things which fit the picture we have.

Now in a safe relationship of the sort I have described, this defensiveness or rigidity, tends to be replaced by an increasing openness to experience. The individual becomes more openly aware of his own feelings and attitudes as they exist in him at an organic level, in the way I tried to describe. He also becomes more aware of reality as it exists outside of himself, instead of perceiving it in preconceived categories. He sees that not all trees are green, not all men are stern fathers, not all women are rejecting, not all failure experiences prove that he is no good, and the like. He is able to take in the evidence in a new situation, *as it is,* rather than distorting it to fit a pattern which he already holds. As you might expect, this increasing ability to be open to experience makes him far more realistic in dealing with new people, new situations, new problems. It means that his beliefs are not rigid, that he can tolerate ambiguity. He can receive much conflicting evidence without forcing closure upon the situation. This openness of awareness to what exists at *this moment* in *oneself* and in *the situation* is, I believe, an important element in the description of the person who emerges from therapy.

Perhaps I can give this concept a more vivid meaning if I illustrate it from a recorded interview. A young professional man reports in the 48th interview the way in which he has become more open to some of his bodily sensations, as well as other feelings.

> *C:* It doesn't seem to me that it would be possible for anybody to relate all the changes that you feel. But I certainly have felt recently that I have more respect for, more objectivity toward my physical makeup. I mean I don't expect too much of myself. This is how it works out: It feels to me that in the past I used to fight a certain tiredness that I felt after supper. Well, now I feel pretty sure that I really *am* tired—that I am not making myself tired—that I am just physiologically lower. It seemed that I was just constantly criticizing my tiredness.
>
> *T:* So you can let yourself *be* tired, instead of feeling along with it a kind of criticism of it.
>
> *C:* Yes, that I shouldn't be tired or something. And it seems in a way to be pretty profound that I can just not fight this tiredness, and along with it goes a real feeling of *I've* got to slow down, too, so that being tired isn't such an awful thing. I think I can also kind of pick up a thread here of why I should be that way in the way my father is and the way he looks at some of these things. For instance, say that I was sick, and I would report this, and it would seem that overtly he would

want to do something about it but he would also communicate, "Oh, my gosh, more trouble." You know, something like that.

T: As though there were something quite annoying really about being physically ill.

C: Yeah, I'm sure that my father has the same disrespect for his own physiology that I have had. Now last summer I twisted my back, I wrenched it, I heard it snap and everything. There was real pain there all the time at first, real sharp. And I had the doctor look at it and he said it wasn't serious, it should heal by itself as long as I didn't bend too much. Well this was months ago—and I have been noticing recently that—hell, this is a real pain and it's still there—and it's not my fault.

T: It doesn't prove something bad about you—

C: No—and one of the reasons I seem to get more tired than I should maybe is because of this constant strain, and so—I have already made an appointment with one of the doctors at the hospital that he would look at it and take an X ray or something. In a way I guess you could say that I am just more accurately sensitive—or objectively sensitive to this kind of thing. . . . And this is really a profound change as I say, and of course my relationship with my wife and the two children is—well, you just wouldn't recognize it if you could see me inside—as you have—I mean—there just doesn't seem to be anything more wonderful than really and genuinely—really *feeling* love for your own children and at the same time receiving it. I don't know how to put this. We have such an increased respect—both of us—for Judy and we've noticed just—as we participated in this—we have noticed such a tremendous change in her—it seems to be a pretty deep kind of thing.

T: It seems to me you are saying that you can listen more accurately to yourself. If your body says it's tired, you listen to it and believe it, instead of criticizing it; if it's in pain, you can listen to that; if the feeling is really loving your wife or children, you can *feel* that, and it seems to show up in the differences in them too.

Here, in a relatively minor but symbolically important excerpt can be seen much of what I have been trying to say about openness to experience. Formerly he could not freely feel pain or illness, because being ill meant being unacceptable. Neither could he feel tenderness and love for his child, because such feelings meant being weak, and he had to maintain his façade of being strong. But now he can be genuinely open to the experiences of his organism—he can be tired when he is tired, he can feel pain when his organism is in pain, he can freely experience the love he feels for his daughter, and he can also feel and express annoyance toward her, as he goes on to say in the next portion of the interview. He can fully live the experiences of his total organism, rather than shutting them out of awareness.

Trust in One's Organism

A second characteristic of the persons who emerge from therapy is difficult to describe. It seems that the person increasingly discovers that his own organism is trustworthy, that it is a suitable instrument for discovering the most satisfying behavior in each immediate situation.

If this seems strange, let me try to state it more fully. Perhaps it will help to understand my description if you think of the individual as faced with some existential choice: "Shall I go home to my family during vacation, or strike out on my own?" "Shall I drink this third cocktail which is being offered?" "Is this the person whom I would like to have as my partner in love and in life?" Thinking of such situations, what seems to be true of the person who emerges from the therapeutic process? To the extent that this person is open to all of his experience, he has access to all of the available data in the situation, on which to base his behavior. He has knowledge of his own feelings and impulses, which are often complex and contradictory. He is freely able to sense the social demands, from the relatively rigid social "laws" to the desires of friends and family. He has access to his memories of similar situations, and the consequences of different behaviors in those situations. He has a relatively accurate perception of this external situation in all of its complexity. He is better able to permit his total organism, his conscious thought participating, to consider, weigh and balance each stimulus, need, and demand, and its relative weight and intensity. Out of this complex weighing and balancing he is able to discover that course of action which seems to come closest to satisfying all his needs in the situation, long-range as well as immediate needs.

In such a weighing and balancing of all of the components of a given life choice, his organism would not by any means be infallible. Mistaken choices might be made. But because he tends to be open to his experience, there is a greater and more immediate awareness of unsatisfying consequences, a quicker correction of choices which are in error.

It may help to realize that in most of us the defects which interfere with this weighing and balancing are that we include things that are not a part of our experience, and exclude elements which are. Thus an individual may persist in the concept that "I can handle liquor," when openness to his past experience would indicate that this is scarcely correct. Or a young woman may see only the good qualities of her prospective mate, where an openness to experience would indicate that he possesses faults as well.

In general then, it appears to be true that when a client is open to his experience, he comes to find his organism more trustworthy. He feels less fear of the emotional reactions which he has. There is a gradual growth of trust in, and even affection for the complex, rich, varied assortment of feelings and tendencies which exist in him at the organic level. Consciousness, instead of being the watchman over a dangerous and unpredictable lot of impulses, of which few can be permitted to see the light of day, becomes the comfortable inhabitant of a society of impulses and feelings and thoughts, which are discovered to be very satisfactorily self-governing when not fearfully guarded.

An Internal Locus or Evaluation

Another trend which is evident in this process of becoming a person relates to the source or locus of choices and decisions, or evaluative judgments. The individual increasingly comes to feel that this locus of evaluation lies within himself. Less and less does he look to others for approval or disapproval; for standards to live by; for decisions and choices. He recognizes that it rests within himself to choose; that the only question which matters is, "Am I living in a way which is deeply satisfying to me, and which truly expresses me?" This I think is perhaps *the* most important question for the creative individual.

Perhaps it will help if I give an illustration. I would like to give a brief portion of a recorded interview with a young woman, a graduate student, who had come for counseling help. She was initially very much disturbed about many problems, and had been contemplating suicide. During the interview one of the feelings she discovered was her great desire to be dependent, just to let someone else take over the direction of her life. She was very critical of those who had not given her enough guidance. She talked about one after another of her professors, feeling bitterly that none of them had taught her anything with deep meaning. Gradually she began to realize that part of the difficulty was the fact that she had taken no initiative in *participating* in these classes. Then comes the portion I wish to quote.

I think you will find that this excerpt gives you some indication of what it means in experience to accept the locus of evaluation as being within oneself. Here then is the quotation from one of the later interviews with this young woman as she has begun to realize that perhaps she is partly responsible for the deficiencies in her own education.

C: Well now, I wonder if I've been going around doing that, getting smatterings of things, and not getting hold, not really getting down to things.

T: Maybe you've been getting just spoonfuls here and there rather than really digging in somewhere rather deeply.

C: M-hm. That's why I say—(*slowly and very thoughtfully*) well, with that sort of a foundation, well, it's really up to *me*. I mean, it seems to be really apparent to me that I *can't depend on someone else* to give me an education. (*Very softly*) I'll really have to get it myself.

T: It really begins to come home—there's only one person that can educate you—a realization that perhaps nobody else *can give* you an education.

C: M-hm. (*Long pause—while she sits thinking*) I have all the symptoms of fright. (*Laughs softly*)

T: Fright? That this is a scary thing, is that what you mean?

C: M-hm. (*Very long pause—obviously struggling with feelings in herself*).

T: Do you want to say any more about what you mean by that? That it really does give you the symptoms of fright?

C: (*Laughs*) I, uh—I don't know whether I quite know. I mean—well it really seems like I'm cut loose (*pause*), and it seems that I'm very—I don't know—in a vulnerable position, but I, uh, I brought this up and it, uh, somehow it almost came out without my saying it. It seems to be—it's something I let out.

T: Hardly a part of you.

C: Well, I felt surprised.

T: As though, "Well for goodness sake, did I say that?" (*Both chuckle.*)

C: Really, I don't think I've had that feeling before. I've—uh, well, this really feels like I'm saying something that, uh, *is* a part of me really. (*Pause*) Or, uh, (*quite perplexed*) it feels like I sort of have, uh, I don't know. I have a feeling of *strength*, and yet, I have a feeling of—realizing it's so sort of fearful, of fright.

T: That is, do you mean that saying something of that sort gives you at the same time a feeling of, of strength in saying it, and yet at the same time a frightened feeling of *what* you have said, is that it?

C: M-hm. I am feeling that. For instance, I'm feeling it internally now—a sort of surging up, or force or outlet. As if that's something really big and strong. And yet, uh, well at first it was almost a physical feeling of just being out alone, and sort of cut off from a—a support I had been carrying around.

T: You feel that it's something deep and strong, and surging forth, and at the same time, you just feel as though you'd cut yourself loose from any support when you say it.

C: M-hm. Maybe that's—I don't know—it's a disturbance of a kind of pattern I've been carrying around, I think.

T: It sort of shakes a rather significant pattern, jars it loose.

C: M-hm. (*Pause, then cautiously, but with conviction*) I, I think—I don't know, but I have the feeling that then I am going to begin to *do* more things that I know I should do. . . . There are so many things that I need to do. It seems in so many avenues of my living I have to work out new ways of behavior, but—maybe—I can see myself doing a little better in some thing.

I hope that this illustration gives some sense of the strength which is experienced in being a unique person, responsible for oneself, and also the uneasiness that accompanies this assumption of responsibility. To recognize that "I am the one who chooses" and "I am the one who determines the value of an experience for me" is both an invigorating and a frightening realization.

Willingness to be a Process

I should like to point out one final characteristic of these individuals as they strive to discover and become themselves. It is that the individual seems to become more content to be a *process* rather than a *product*. When he enters the therapeutic relationship, the client is likely to wish to achieve some fixed state: he wants to reach the point where his problems are solved, or where he is effective in his work, or where his marriage is satisfactory. He tends, in the freedom of the therapeutic relationship to drop such fixed goals, and to accept a more satisfying realization that he is not a fixed entity, but a process of becoming.

Our client, at the conclusion of therapy, says in rather puzzled fashion, "I haven't finished the job of integrating and reorganizing myself, but that's only confusing, not discouraging, now that I realize this is a continuing process. . . . It's exciting, sometimes up-setting, but deeply encouraging to feel yourself in action, apparently knowing where you are going even though you don't always consciously know where that is." One can see here both the expression of trust in the organism, which I have mentioned, and also the realiza-tion of self as a process. Here is a personal description of what it seems like to accept oneself as a stream of becoming, not a finished product. It means that a person is a fluid process, not a fixed and static entity; a flowing river of change, not a block of solid material; a continually changing constellation of potentialities, not a fixed quantity of traits.

Here is another statement of this same element of fluidity or existential living, "This whole train of experiencing, and the meanings that I have thus far discovered in it, seem to have launched me on a process which is both fascinating and at times a little frighten-ing. It seems to mean letting my experiences carry me on, in a direction which appears to be forward, towards goals that I can but dimly define, as I try to understand at least the current meaning of that experience. The sensation is that of floating with a complex stream of experience, with the fascinating possibility of trying to comprehend its ever-changing complexity."

Conclusion

I have tried to tell you what has seemed to occur in the lives of people with whom I have had the privilege of being in a relationship as they struggled toward becoming themselves. I have endeavored to describe, as accurately as I can, the meanings which seem to be involved in this process of becoming a person. I am sure that this process is *not* one that occurs only in therapy. I am sure that I do not see it clearly or completely, since I keep changing my comprehension and understanding of it. I hope you will accept it as a current and tentative picture, not as something final.

One reason for stressing the tentative nature of what I have said is that I wish to make it clear that I am *not* saying, "This is what you should become; here is the goal for you." Rather, I am saying that these are some of the meanings I see in the experiences that my clients and I have shared. Perhaps this picture of the experience of others may illuminate or give more meaning to some of your own experience.

I have pointed out that each individual appears to be asking a double question: "Who am I?" and "How may I become myself?" I have stated that in a favorable psychological climate a process of becoming takes place; that here the individual drops one after another of the defensive masks with which he has faced life; that he experiences fully the hidden aspects of himself; that he discovers in these experiences the stranger who has been living behind these masks, the stranger who is himself. I have tried to give my picture of the characteristic attributes of the person who emerges; a person who is more open to all of the elements of his organic experience; a person who is developing a trust in his own organism as an instrument of sensitive living; a person who accepts the locus of evaluation as residing within himself; a person who is learning to live in his life as a participant in a fluid, ongoing process, in which he is continually discovering new aspects of himself in the flow of his experience. These are some of the elements which seem to me to be involved in becoming a person.

6. Can an Adult Change?

Robert L. Sutherland

Can an adult change? If so, why should he, and how can he! Such questions go beyond findings of the scientist. Even the philosopher or poet has difficulty answering them.

At one time these questions seemed easier to answer than they do now. Modern industry, so accustomed to applying science to technology, once hoped that it could find a blueprint or slide-rule for people. Management and personnel workers asked the psychiatrist and psychologist for quick and ready rules of thumb: tests with numerical results, personality profiles with clear pictures, and procedures for assuring high morale among groups.

Experts in human behavior have found some answers, and are adding more. Psychiatrists probe with insight; psychologists appraise with accuracy; social psychologists and sociologists subject intra- and inter-group relations to experimental research. But even with present measures, personality remains complex, rich, varied, and, to some extent, unpredictable.

Students of human nature themselves are now turning from easily isolated traits and abilities to the more baffling areas of basic motives and of inter-personal relations. The United States Air Force found that choosing a bomber crew because of their separate and

From *Understanding Mental Health: A Common Need, A Less Frequent Achievement* by R.L. Sutherland and B.K. Smith, Van Nostrand Reinhold Company, New York, 1965. Permission granted by The Hogg Foundation for Mental Health and the author.

specialized aptitudes brought together qualified individuals but did not produce a functioning team. If the sparks of motive and morale were missing, individual talents were of little use.

Brown and Holtzman, in their study habits inventory, report the same to be true in academic life.[1] A strong desire for learning far outweighs any particular method of study. Dr. James S. Plant also said this in his psychiatric work: Let me know first what a person is really after—his goals—and I will then be interested in your measurement of his intelligence, skills, and knowledge.[2] Spriegel and Bailey likewise acknowledge that the motives of people determine whether or not a logical plan of management will work.[3]

If one accepts as moderately sound the premise just stated, he can proceed with the subject at hand which, disturbingly enough, is himself! How can a person understand his own attitudes, the motives which underlie them, and the social roles he plays? And harder still—how can he change them? Or does he need to? Or, is he too old to! Or can he acquire new skills, interests, and attitudes without probing the old, mercilessly?

Need for Change

A person of high status may hate to admit a weakness, for fear that change will undermine his position. An "unsuccessful person" may be threatened still more by a full realization of his inadequacies. Or, conversely, the "successful person" may feel so secure that further change and development are not a threat but a challenge. Moreover, an unsuccessful person may be goaded to new effort by his failures. Thus, there are many pros and cons to the question of whether an adult

---

[1] William F. Brown and Wayne H. Holtzman, "Use of the Survey of Study Habits and Attitudes for Counseling Students," *Personnel and Guidance Journal*, vol. 35, no. 4, December, 1956, pp. 214-218.

[2] This idea was expressed by Dr. James S. Plant in addresses given in Texas. The same point of view is demonstrated in his books, *Personality and the Cultural Pattern*, The Commonwealth Fund, New York, 1937; and *The Envelope, A Study of the Impact of the World Upon the Child*, The Commonwealth Fund, New York, 1950.

[3] See William Robert Spriegel and Joseph Kenneth Bailey, "The Staff Function in Organization," *Advanced Management*, March, 1952, pp. 2-6.

can or should change. As we shall see later, the concept of self is one of the important factors.

Luckily, not much change is needed. Most adults are not in mental and correctional institutions! Even the troubled person who goes to the psychiatrist is given assurance that he need not condemn himself and undergo complete change. Adults, in the main, have been moderately successful in family life, at work, and in community affairs—some remarkably so. Furthermore, they live in a democracy which tolerates and even encourages individuality—a wide range of behavior.[4]

The confident speaker of a few years ago who could reel off characteristics of the successful leader in community affairs or business, now acknowledges that many different kinds of people are functioning effectively. Attention has shifted to the roles and functions of leaders and to the variety of contributions different individuals can make to a group. Parents do not try to shape their several children by a single mold. Individuality and difference in outcome are expected and desired.

Not only is little change needed, but usually not too much is possible, though each person is capable of some. The psychiatrist knows that adults are not entirely rigid, but they are rather firmly put together. "Integrated" is the word for it. What they are has developed over many years. Personality arises out of need and out of one's unique experiences from infancy. An adult cannot put his personality aside and take on another any more than he can jump out of his skin. Many people, nevertheless, want to progress in their development. They hope to do better than "tolerably well," even if they cannot reach for the moon. If this desire for continued change and improvement is already one of the possessions of human beings, how can they carry it out? Before this is answered, the prior question is: When does a person need to change—for the better?

---

[4]William H. Whyte, Jr., to the contrary notwithstanding. Note his fear of stereotyped Americans in *The Organization Man,* Simon and Schuster, New York, 1956.

Slight Danger Signals

No one can give a dogmatic answer, nor can science. The following tentative suggestions as to when and why an adult might consider change came from clinicians, industrial supervisors, and teachers, who appreciate individual variation but who also realize that adult personalities need to grow.

The most that can be said is that the person who behaves in several of the following ways might suspect that a little change is in order.[5] Not much, just a little! Let us call it continuous development or, as Gordon Allport says, "becoming."[6] Here are some of the signals:

Resisting change—An adult may suspect that he needs to change a bit if he finds that he strongly resists change. The one who resents suggestions, hold to his present ways defensively, and clings to a status quo which itself is outdated, is letting himself become so rigid that he cannot change if he has to. Perhaps there is some virtue in a little change for its own sake as one goes along. This is especially true in a turbulent society in which today's status quo has already changed by tomorrow.

A person can be flexible, humble, and searching, without being blown by the wind. A balance is needed between steadfastness of purpose and lack of bullheadedness—between determination to reach a goal and an ability to work with others to attain it.

Systematizing everything—An individual may suspect that a little change is indicated if he discovers that he is getting most of his emotional satisfaction out of a minor virtue, like orderliness. Systematizing things and people is usually thought of as desirable—and it is—but like many other good traits, it can be overdone. Some

---

[5] As Mr. Hardin Smith has pointed out, a person cannot always see and evaluate his own behavior patterns. Because people have difficulty in seeing themselves as they are, management trainers and other applied social psychologists have developed various group techniques intended to help the individual see himself as others see him. (Mr. Smith's ideas were developed in an unpublished commentary on the management seminars which he directed for Southwestern Bell Telephone Co.)

[6] Gordon Allport, *Becoming,* Yale University Press, New Haven, 1956.

people who are slaves to their intricate systems and want others to follow suit rigidly, may be dodging the bigger responsibility of granting freedom and initiative to others, even freedom to make their own mistakes. Perfectionism, domination, and oversupervision are word-fellows of close kin.

Being an "unorganizer"—A person may need to change if he represents the other extreme—if he is a disorganizer, an unorganizer; if he flutters and clutters when things are awry but clings to his state of confusion. He looks bothered; he is baffled; he yearns for peace and order, but he has not learned to achieve it. He can, though—possibly!

Resenting evaluation—He may need to change if he does well the work of the day but resists and resents evaluation. He shies from big ideas and clings to busy work. He likes to dictate letters and especially inter-office memoranda but avoids the assigned task of developing a five-year plan with his department. He thwarts himself and others who need to cope with the future.

Dreaming—and more dreaming—On the other hand, if he only dreams and never touches reality, he is first revered as an "idea man" only to be discounted later as a visionary who has lost his sense of proportion and of reality.

Damning things—and sometimes people—Some change would help if he finds himself spending much of his time and still more of his emotional energy in damning somebody or something—the Republicans, the Democrats, his company, his job, his community, his competitor, his government, another nationality, race, or religion. Now, all of these need to be criticized, for none is perfect. But a constant habit of criticism develops a sour look, a dour countenance, a permanent furrow in the brow, a voice with a high pitch, or low whine. Negativism, suspicion, and fear can become personality habits quite as much as any other attitude.

Worrying—for the "fun" of it—A person may suspect that change is needed if he is a "worrier." He may know that worry uses up whatever it is that the internal glands of secretion produce, and that this is bad for the heart and the liver. But, feeling lonesome without worry, he keeps right on worrying. Then, as if to compound the bad interest, he worries about his habit of worrying. It becomes a vicious cycle, but also an emotionally pleasant one, in a pathological sort of way.

Worry, of course, cannot be dismissed with a turn of the phrase; it is often a symptom of an underlying problem to which the psychoanalyst might give years of attention, or it may be somewhat more superficial—a behavior pattern carried on more as a matter of habit after the original problem was solved or outlived.

Sarcasm—for the "sting" of it—Dropping to a lesser problem than worrying, a person may need to change if he is a sarcastic soul. He may know that sarcasm has low utility in human relations; but if he has the habit, he keeps on practicing it. There are two kinds of sarcastic digs: The one made in the presence of another person is often said with a smile as a matter of defense; the other dig, made behind one's back, is often more extreme, sullen, and self-righteous.

Nagging—If a person is a nagger, a wire recording of his voice might make him horrified at his own tenseness, unattractive manner, and authoritarian air, but he is likely to repeat the same behavior the next day. Oversupervision may be a form of nagging and vice-versa.

Procrastinating—The one who covers up indecision and procrastination by thinking he is being democratic—that is, conferring with every Tom, Dick, and Sally before acting—needs to look at his rationalization more rationally! The desire to include others in planning is admirable; the humility which permits a person to seek advice is desirable; but the one who queries others must not forget that he, himself, is a person—not just a mirror of other people's fears, ideas, and hopes. If there is some direction to his life, some consistency to his planning, and skill in using earlier experience, he has a mind of his own, capable of figuring out a line of action, even in a new situation. He confers with others, but also with himself!

Making Quick Decisions—The opposite of the pro-crastinator may be still harder to live with. The "decisive one" has a mind that clicks, and has a yen for action. In the back of his mind is the picture of an efficient administrator who glances at a problem, sizes it up in a jiffy, and issues a memorandum about its solution before his first thought is dry. He gets things done all right, but, sadly, they often have to be undone. His desire for results makes him insensitive and roughshod. His self confidence makes him authoritarian and unconcerned about achieving a consensus of opinion among his co-workers who may have a right to be in on the decision and whose cooperation is needed in the action. Can he slow up a bit? Can he develop some empathy, where now there is only compulsion? Can his enthusiasm for a goal be tempered without being curbed? Can he change a little, but remain basically himself, the kind of person without whom little would ever get done? We think so.

Running for shelter—The person who by virtue of his managerial or professional position is expected to be helpful to others, but who runs from their problems, is in need of change. Subconsciously, he wants to avoid becoming entangled in another's emotional situation because he is a confused or immature person himself. There are various defenses: He is in too big a hurry to sit down and listen; his efficient secretary keeps the flow of calls and callers moving so fast that no one is at ease to state a problem; he holds people off through the red tape of forms, memoranda, and carbon copies. Persons who come to him leave with their original problem unheeded; in addition, they feel frustrated, apologetic, and guilty for having bothered him. How can this person come to see what he is really doing to others? How can he be the leader of an organization administratively, and be available to hear the human problems which inevitably arise in any large group? This is his dilemma, but because of his own emotional problems, he fails to face it, and, instead, has learned to run and to hide!

Making frankness a fetish—Now, what about the person who rests on his honesty? He is so impressed with the importance of what he thinks of as frankness that he may confuse it with cruelty. He considers himself a straight shooter. Such "honesty" can cause him to be hard on himself through condemnation. But he gets still more excitement out of being daringly frank with and watching the pained reactions of others. He is so self-righteous about giving the other person a quick inventory of his faults that the victim is caught off guard and may not fight back. Before our "virtuous" one gets through with his attack he has expressed not so much the high ethics of honesty as aggression in the form of psychological sadism.

Wearing feelings on the proverbial sleeve—Then there is the overly suspicious and sensitive person. Can he develop a little more faith and confidence in others and a slightly thicker skin on himself? In his presence, one has to weigh everything said lest it be taken personally. The sensitive one is quick to fly off the handle because he reads malice into the action of others. His blood pressure rises in self-defense, but how silly is a show of defense when there is no attack!

Can he view life less personally, more objectively? His suspicious tendencies are not superficial, but may reflect an insecurity tracing back to the usual place. Nevertheless, trying a new skill—that of acting toward others as though they were friendly—can lead to some change and can mean success in proving that others are cooperative.

For more persistent problems, psychotherapy, or at least group psychotherapy, may be needed. But new types of group experience, to be discussed later, may bring out a favorable response in more superficial cases.

Clinging to well-earned status—"What is the most common human relations difficulty you encounter?" When this question was asked the head of a firm which specializes in psychological counseling to top management, the answer was unequivocal. "One can always expect the problem of the leader who was responsible for developing the company in the early days but now cannot give up authority and status roles to younger, possibly more able, junior executives," the head of the firm replied. "The man kills himself with overwork, while the junior executives lose interest."

Industry is not the only place where one finds the uneasy person who tries to hold on to the status and responsibility he has earned. "The sense of being replaced" is a hard one to cope with in movie and television stardom, in business, in civic responsibility, and also in the family as children grow up and form families of their own. It is not made easier when the newcomer fails to recognize the accomplishments and continued value of the older leader and thinks of himself as the bright and shining hope of a bogged-down organization.

The problem is compounded by the attention which others give the new person and the new ideas he brings. The older one forgets that he enjoyed this acceptance at one time and that life moves on. Stepping down in responsibility has never been easy for persons living in our competitive culture. There are ways of doing it, ways of preparing for it, new types of service one can render, and even new forms of satisfaction in the expansion and success of the program and of the younger personnel in it. Such a shift in attitude and situation "takes some doing," does not come from simple advice, self-given or otherwise. It is one aspect of the total problem of preparation for retirement which might better be phrased "preparation for continuous growth."

Personality Was Not "Built" in a Day

Complete change is difficult because, as we have mentioned before, the person's present way of living has a long history. While he may be aware of the high points, the underlying determinants of his behavior are a mystery to him. From birth, every individual is a dynamic, striving, interacting, wanting organism; but the exact nature of his goals and the way he achieves them are not pre-determined. The culture in which he is reared has much to do with what goals he will seek and the paths he will take.

Interwoven also are his early inter-personal experiences of success and failure in the family and in other close associations. Quite accidentally a child may hit upon a mode of behavior which brings a favorable response. Without realizing it, he plays the same role when a similar situation arises. And, if the person who reacts satisfactorily is one whose love and support he very much needs, then the role becomes well confirmed.

We say that children have devious ways of getting what they want or of avoiding what they dislike. We are amazed at the subtlety of their approach. These "ways" are purposeful and experimental. The process is so sensitive and indirect that even the adult may not know just how he has influenced the child. The best word for it is social interaction. Throughout his lifetime a person interacts with his social environment, especially with the response of his intimate associates. He is constantly changing, developing, becoming creative, remaining rigid, fearful, withdrawn, or defensive—depending upon the unique combination of experiences through which he has lived and the way his personality has developed in their presence.

Identical twins have the same genetic make-up and come from the same environment, but each is a distinctive personality. Slight variation in the meaning of an experience, or a small difference in the attitude of a parent toward a child colors his reaction. In a family of five or even ten children, parents may say they treat all alike, but they are the first to acknowledge that they really do not, and that each child is different. Children in the same family have varying influences on one another, on their parents, and in the neighborhood.

Approaches to Change

Since the subtleties of development are obscure, even to the person himself, change becomes a process, not merely an easy response to a simple wish. Anyone who wants to start moving in a different direction had better take off, not at jet-speed, but at a slow pace and alter his course only a few degrees. Drastic change has been recorded in religious conversion, but for most persons, slow, consistent development is more feasible than sudden transitions.

Is insight a necessary first step?—Is clear insight into one's present nature and the problems he faces a prerequisite to change? This simple question could lead to an involved argument! Let us look at those who take

the affirmative; in a later section the negative will be
stated. The psychoanalyst may work with the patient
from one to five hours a week for several months or
years, helping him unravel his emotional past as a
prelude to understanding his present. With such insight
and with the supporting help of the therapist, the
patient can marshal his resources for continued growth.
He can start playing a slightly different role and enjoy
the emotional satisfaction of successful change which
tends to confirm the new trend in his development.

Brief psychotherapy and group psychotherapy also
help a person understand himself. And, with the
sympathetic encouragement of the therapist or the
group, the person can change a bit at first and more
later.

All persons in the "helping professions" know the
importance of good listening as a way of encouraging a
person to talk out his problem and gain insight into
himself. The social caseworker is trained in it. The nurse
and doctor establish rapport with the patient by
observing his moods and listening to his concerns. The
clinical psychologist practices it. All therapists in a
rehabilitation team are instructed as much in sensitivity
to the patient as in the content of their own specialty.
The industrial personnel worker, the military chaplain,
and the civilian minister are often called upon to serve
as counselors.

Most people do not have benefit of therapy or even
of general counseling. For many of us, just the normal
process of growing up is accompanied by some insight
and awareness of choice. From our ordinary experiences, we catch glimpses of ourselves by noticing,
almost without realizing it, the reaction of others to
what we do. In this indirect way, people with whom we
associate mirror and evaluate the nature which we have
expressed. If we admire the persons with whom we
associate and whose reactions we glimpse, we are
especially influenced by their responses. This "looking
glass self" process is subtle, it is social, and it is
effective.[7] Even in our memory we play through the

---

[7]Charles Horton Cooley, *Human Nature and the Social Order,* The Free
Press, Glencoe, Illinois, Revised edition, 1956, pp. 183-184.

roles of the day, gaining a clearer view of what we have done and of how our better selves, our better friends, or our religious ideal might judge our progress.

Listening to a symphony or a good sermon or identifying with characters in a play may also aid an adult to gain insight. Or, as his mind wanders during a leisurely day of fishing or hiking, or just plain loafing, he may acquire a perspective and return to look at a problem or a relationship in a different light.

Hobbies, sports, vacations, are thought of as refreshing not merely because they stimulate one through the use of different muscles and interests, not merely because they relax one who is tense from worry or fatigue, but also because they are conducive to obtaining new perspectives. One can focus on a problem just so long. He can face it frankly, gather facts about it, plan alternative strategies. These are all-important plodding stages in the process of problem-solving. But, often a new synthesis which illumines the stolid facts may intrude itself gently in his consciousness during a day of relaxation. The art of creative thought and the nature of insight are not entirely mysterious. Numerous books have been written and experiments conducted.[8]

Is "accentuating the positive" an aid or an illusion?— If one side of the argument says that insight into one's problem is a prerequisite to change, the other side is that a perennial quest for insight may lead to morbid introspection. There is, indeed, a difference between the two. Insight can be about anything, including oneself. It is merely a concept, a unifying idea, which brings meaning to an array of facts.

Introspection, on the other hand, is a more emotionally loaded term which always refers to one's inward look. The person engaging in introspection dwells upon his past, trying to diagnose his present. Insight is synonymous with any creative thought, while introspection may lead either to inspired outpourings of a

---

[8] Alex F. Osborn, *Applied Imagination,* Charles Scribner's Sons, New York, 1953. Clarence E. Winland, "Creative Thought in Scientific Research," *Scientific Monthly,* LXXV, No. 6, December, 1952, p. 352. J.P. Guilford, "Creativity," *American Psychologist,* September, 1950, pp. 444-454.

great poet or to the distortions and depression of
inveterate self-analysis. Chained to a bothersome past,
such a person has difficulty facing the future with
creative imagination, a light touch, and buoyant determination.

Rather than dust off all the skeletons in our private
closet, most of us need to accept *who* we are and *what*
we are with good grace and humor, just as we accept our
children and our colleagues with all of their differences
and even their faults. This does not gloss over imper-
fections, but neither does it blind one with their glare.
In successful change, one should be more conscious of
his good qualities than of his deficiencies, of his
accomplishments than of his failures. With this sense of
balance and assurance, he finds it much easier to
confront himself with an awareness of weakness and
find ways of increasing present strengths and acquiring
new ones.[9]

Looking, then, at the future, the all-important step in
change is to start behaving in a more emotionally
satisfying way. It takes intelligence and imagination to
see and try a new pattern.

For example, the poorest way to change is to say, "I
will stop over-supervising others; I will stop being
negative; I will stop being disorganized; I will stop being
sarcastic, pessimistic, or perfectionistic to a fault." In
freshman grammar we learned that two negatives make a
positive, but psychologically this seldom happens.

Can a more satisfying way be found?—On the other
hand, if one can find a more emotionally rewarding new
way, he is well on the road to change. The chronic
oversupervisor may one time experience the still more
subtle satisfaction of seeing another person accomplish a
goal on his own. This time the supervisor obtains real
pleasure in his own restraint. He shares vicariously the
other person's accomplishment, and his mind starts

---

[9]Many techniques exist for helping a person to see himself as he looks
to others. This "mirroring" can be done in role playing, small group
discussion, through the use of recording devices and playbacks, in
unstructured "training group" sessions, and in case-moderating discussions.
(Some of these methods were mentioned by Mr. Hardin Smith in the
reference mentioned previously.)

working on other ways to release the creative ability in his co-workers. The new morale of the group is reward itself.

The one who does today what he would normally put off 'til next month surprises himself pleasantly! It will be still easier for him to make the same "mistake" again; and before he knows it, he will be experiencing an inner satisfaction in punctuality. It is really not this easy, but there is something in the admonition: To be different, one must start acting differently and experience the reward of new emotional satisfactions. It takes ingenuity to discover a new pattern which will be both more efficient socially and more satisfying emotionally. The intelligent person not too burdened with restraining emotions can do it. But the fearful, suspicious, and otherwise deeply insecure and disturbed person clings to the old pattern, poor though it is, for this clinging gives him a sense of security, false though it is. A crisis, long-term psychotherapy, or some other basic emotional experience may have to come before change occurs.

New skills are tools—Acquiring new skills in human relations is held by some social psychologists to be of great importance. They pay little attention to the insight-prelude to change which we have described, nor do they emphasize psychoanalysis with its special way of focusing on the emotional past with its conflicts, fears, and sense of inadequacy.

Rather, they look to the present and the future. They believe that if one acquires new skills which help him overcome or go around or even live with a problem, the problem itself shrinks in importance. The positive approach is to find a better way—not to worry about a mistake. "Skill training" is their answer. Practice new ways of working with others through role playing and other small group devices, is their suggestion. Invent and try new patterns of committee work, decision-making, of "feeding back" ideas from a subcommittee to a larger group, of arriving at a consensus, of highlighting group findings—these are the tools of those who stress the forward look in human relations. They think they can help the individual get promoted out of or beyond a problem without enlarging its importance by clinging to it agonizingly long.

They have something. They would agree that to acknowledge and use this new approach does not mean to abandon others. What they have is useful regardless of how one combines it with other forms of help. Their emphasis upon inventing new skills in human relations is a positive approach. The individual, as he uses these skills, experiences a sense of release from the past and of enthusiasm for the future because he has found more successful ways of reaching his goal.

There is a fancy word for it!—Another approach to change is sometimes called "milieu therapy."[10] The commonplace technique consists of joining a small, intimate, high morale group whose members are already moving in the direction one wants to go. A young adult long confirmed in the negative wit of sarcasm, gained insight into the problem through several of the methods already discussed, including counseling, but a year later was relatively unchanged in spite of a strong desire for improvement. He decided to try a change in milieu by moving from the rarified atmosphere of the pseudo-intellectuals with whom he had been living and quietly joining a residential group with different, more open, more positive outlook and yet with similar intellectual capacity. Without too much direct awareness, he found himself taking on a more friendly role. It was the pattern prevalent around him. It was the behavior condoned and rewarded by the approval of his new associates.

The subtle influence on one's self when he plays a role like that being played by others around him may be the indirect, social way in which imitation operates effectively. One takes on and becomes a part of any role to which he gives his loyalty and interest. When he chooses a certain milieu, he internalizes the values and patterns of the group almost unwittingly. It is not an

---

[10]David McK. Rioch and Alfred H. Stanton, "Milieu Therapy," *Psychiatry*, vol. 16, 1953, pp. 65-72. Republished from: *Proceedings of the Association for Research in Nervous and Mental Disease*, Vol. XXXI, 1953. See also Ruth Barnard, "Milieu Therapy," *Menninger Quarterly*, vol. 8 No. (2), 1954, pp. 20-24.

all-encompassing function because he plays other roles as well, including some carryover of his former way, but there is a chance for change.

The importance of the small group in personality development was stressed by sociologists long before group dynamics gave it not only a new theoretical importance but a laboratory procedure for research and for controlled influence on persons. One of the leading journals in the sociological field has devoted an issue to the topic of the small group.[11] Industrial management has a similar emphasis. *Motivation: the Core of Management* summarizes research which shows that the morale of the small group and the rapport of the group leader with the members are two most important factors in productivity, even more important than the enlightened policies of top management.[12]

Milieu therapy has found its way clinically into hospitals and other medical settings. Management has become convinced of its importance, and the social psychologist, the sociologist, and the everyday person have also discovered its importance.

The teacher is the learner—An effective approach to change in oneself is to help another person in his development. While one is focusing on the other fellow, he is unwittingly confirming a trend in his own growth. Long considered axiomatic is the statement that a person really learns only after he himself becomes the teacher. Religion affirms that a person develops spiritually when he helps others toward salvation. He finds himself only when he loses himself in a cause greater than himself.

Similarly, counselors learn most about themselves after they begin counseling. It is then that their supervisors find them aware of their own needs and ready for change. Many persons have been attracted to the "helping professions" because of their own emotional problems. This factor is not necessarily a handicap. If such persons have worked their way through

---

[11] *American Sociological Review,* Vol. 19, No. 6, Dec., 1954.

[12] *Motivation: the Core of Management,* Personnel Series No. 155, American Management Association, New York, 1953.

their own difficulties, they may have greater insight and a more sympathetic approach than the stolid ones who were never aware of need. Psychoanalysis follows the same line of reasoning. No one is certified to practice until he himself has undergone analysis and then has helped out others under controlled supervision.

Self-reliance and independence aid in change—A person who has acquired a realistic view of himself and who has developed new skills in human relations acquires confidence in the future and a certain detachment from immediate vicissitudes. This feeling of independence enables him to judge his own progress and to set still higher goals. He is not dependent on others for daily nods of approval and other forms of recognition, nor does he need the limelight of public opinion as a gauge of his success. He now knows who he is, where he wants to go, and what consistent progress he can make. He realizes that a husband, a wife, an admiring friend, a minister, or psychiatrist can be a helpful reinforcement, but also that he should not be completely dependent on any one of them.

We all have the spark of nobility—The final phase of growth is an undergirding of the others. One can change in particulars more easily if he acquires appropriate basic or generalized attitudes such as open-mindedness, a belief in the goodness of human nature, a faith in the future, and a confident relationship to whatever he defines as eternal. Religionists and educators have long talked in these terms; more recently, industrialists have joined them in discovering that in the least of us there is a spark of nobility, that most of us not only can rise above the motive of intelligent selfishness to a higher order of living, if encouraged, but that we yearn to do so.

Yes, change in an adult is possible. Continuous growth and life itself can become synonymous.

Reading Suggestions

Two popular articles, featured nationally, deal with topics similar to those discussed in this paper. They are:

"How to Live with Job Pressure," Robert H. Felix, *Nation's Business,* September, 1956, pp. 38-39, 85-87. Reprints may be

obtained for ten cents a copy or $7.50 per 100, postpaid, from
Nation's Business, 1615 H. Street, N.W., Washington 6, D.C.

How to Deal With Your Tensions, George S. Stevenson, published
by the National Association for Mental Health, 1957. Available without cost from Better Mental Health, Box 2500, New
York 1, New York.

Two other excellent articles which discuss business and human
relations are:

"Managers Need Three Smart Teachers," John Corson, *Nation's
Business,* January, 1957, pp. 78-82. Reprints may be obtained
for fifteen cents a copy or $11.25 per 100, postpaid, from
Nation's Business, 1615 H. Street, N.W., Washington 6, D.C.

"Faith in a Creative Society," Abram T. Collier, *Harvard Business
Review,* May-June, 1957, pp. 35-41.

7. The Place of Affective Learning

Earl C. Kelley

I was pleased to be invited to write this editorial because the topic for this month is of the utmost importance. It could well come about that this is one of the most important issues in the history of this publication.

The reason for this statement is that it has now become abundantly clear, from research and from reason, that *how a person feels is more important than what he knows.* This seems true because how one feels controls behavior, while what one knows does not. What one knows is used in behavior, to be sure, but the way it is used depends upon positive or negative feelings. It is possible to be a saint or a demon with similar knowledge. History furnishes ample illustrations of knowledge being put to evil uses. The Nazis who slaughtered six million innocent people knew too much but felt too little.

We in education are slowly waking up to the fact that feelings are really important. This can be seen in educational literature. There is much discussion of the self-concept, the self-image, and of the fact that if one thinks too little of himself he becomes immobile and unable to learn. In fact, the person who has come to hate himself and others does not take in much subject matter.

Educational Leadership 22: 455-457; April 1965. Reprinted with permission of the Association for Supervision and Curriculum Development and Earl C. Kelley. Copyright © 1965 by the Association for Supervision and Curriculum Development.

All of this causes us to take another look at subject matter and its uses. None of the above is to imply that what one knows is not important. One's proper subject matter is the universe around him, and without some comprehension of that universe and his relation to it, he could not know how to deal with it, no matter how he felt.

Subject matter and feeling are so closely intertwined that they can no longer be considered a duality. Everyone who learns something has some feeling about it, and so, as in so many other areas, they are inseparable. No matter what we do, affective learning goes on anyway. When this affective learning is positive, the learner becomes constructive in his behavior.

We need to reconsider our ideas and attitudes toward subject matter itself. It has long been considered an end in itself. If the learner came through in possession of a large store of subject matter, we have said he is "good." If the subject matter was something the learner could not or would not store, and be able to prove that he had stored it, he has been considered "bad," or at least a failure.

We ought to be able to reconsider the role of subject matter. It is not a question of reducing the importance of what is learned, but of seeing the relationship between accumulated information and the unique learner. I have on occasion been charged with not wanting learners to learn anything, but only to feel good. This is not true. One of my basic criticisms of the traditional school is that those in attendance do not learn nearly enough. We have reared a generation of people who have been schooled but not educated.

The main reason for this outcome is that with our rigorous subject matter approach we have closed personalities when we should have been opening them. We have used fear and anxiety as motivating devices, and this has repelled the learner when we should have been attracting him. When the learner has not, because of these destructive feelings, learned what we adults purpose him to learn, we have had to resort to coercion of one form or another. Coercion sets in motion a whole cycle of negative affects, often resulting in open hostility and rejection on the part of both learner and teacher. Many such learners are then headed toward the human scrap-heap—the rejects known as dropouts, the educationally disinherited, who in most cases will be unable to cope with the society of the future. It is from this human scrap-heap that most of our delinquent and mentally ill are drawn.

The basic error in most of our curriculum work is that we start with the materials, which are the tools of education, not the product. We choose our tools first, and then look around to see what we are going to do with them. These materials are usually chosen without regard to the individual differences among the learners, often without regard to the culture of the community where the school is located. Curriculum building is the only operation I know about where the tool is chosen before what is to be built is known or decided upon.

We have for so long chosen the curriculum with little regard for the feelings of the learner that we are of course unskilled in planning curriculum with affect in mind. When new understandings show us that how a person feels is more important than what he knows, our old assumptions and procedures will no longer suffice. We are faced with a requirement to learn new methods of using materials. If we had spent as much time on considering the feelings of the learner as we have in choosing and presenting information, we would by now know how to go about it.

We cannot say that, although planning curriculum with affective learning in mind is a clear necessity, we do not know how to do it, and so we will continue to ignore it. Since such planning is a requirement, we will have to learn how to do it, just as any other workman must do when his past methods have become obsolete.

Getting Started

I cannot of course tell others how to do this. Each school system and each individual teacher must solve this problem in his own way, taking into account his own resources, the nature of his unique learners and the community in which he works. I can, however, make a few general suggestions which may provide a way of getting started.

Many schools have committees which work on curriculum. Every school needs some organization of this sort. A school cannot in these changing times continue to operate well without somebody examining what is being done, and what ought to be done in the light of new evidence and new conditions. Even in a factory someone has to spend some of his time in planning.

I would like to see such a committee not address itself to the material first, since this has been done many times. I would like the committee members to ask themselves a new set of questions.

How can we secure commitment to the learning task on the part of our learners? *Educational Leadership* had a whole issue on commitment recently, and some articles on the topic even splashed over into another issue. I know of no way to get anybody committed to any task anywhere without consultation and some choice. This raises another question.

What are the ways of bringing about consultation and some choice with the learner? In other words, how go about teacher-pupil planning, so that what is to be done makes some sense to the learner? There is a rich supply of literature in this field.

How can we take advantage of the learner's uniqueness, rather than considering it a handicap?

How can we give the academically gifted a chance to use his ability without depriving him of many of his peers? In our own form of segregation, the gifted are actually deprived.

How can we make available to the learner his proper subject matter, which is not alone held in a book but consists of the whole world around him?

What shall we do about marks? Do they on the whole bring about more negative than positive feeling?

What are our devices for rejection, and how may they be reduced?

These are only a few of the questions which might be raised. Any committee sensitive to the feelings of learners will find more. Eventually, after all of these questions are effectively dealt with, the committee will finally come to this one: What materials shall we use, and how shall we use them?

I have a strong belief that every learner should feel better, more able to cope with unknown vicissitudes, more courageous at the end of a class than he did at the opening. If he feels worse, less able and less courageous, then the class has damaged him, rather than helped him. If this is oft repeated then he is on his way to the human scrap-heap.

I further strongly believe that if a teacher behaves in such a way as to open selves, open personalities, and then has something around for people to learn, they will learn. And this learning will be greater in quantity and in usefulness than would be the case if learners are driven to close themselves. We cannot open selves and render them receptive if we start our classes with threats.

The future must appear promising, not threatening, if learners are to come toward the teacher rather than retreat from him. The learner must have confidence in the teacher, feel that there is no double-cross in prospect, before he can open up. This confidence is not conveyed alone by what we say but mostly by our behavior.

8. Significant Learning: In Therapy and Education

Carl R. Rogers

Presented here is a thesis, a point of view, regarding the implications which psychotherapy has for education. It is a stand which I take tentatively, and with some hesitation. I have many unanswered questions about this thesis. But it has, I think, some clarity in it, and hence it may provide a starting point from which clear differences can emerge.

Significant Learning in Psychotherapy

Let me begin by saying that my long experience as a therapist convinces me that significant learning is facilitated in psychotherapy, and occurs in that relationship. By significant learning I mean learning which is more than an accumulation of facts. It is learning which makes a difference—in the individual's behavior, in the course of action he chooses in the future, in his attitudes and in his personality. It is a pervasive learning which is not just an accretion of knowledge, but which interpenetrates with every portion of his existence.

Now it is not only my subjective feeling that such learning takes place. This feeling is substantiated by research. In client-centered therapy, the orientation with which I am most familiar, and in which the most research has been done, we know that exposure to such therapy produces learnings, or changes, of these sorts:

The person comes to see himself differently.

He accepts himself and his feelings more fully.

He becomes more self-confident and self-directing.

He becomes more the person he would like to be.

He becomes more flexible, less rigid, in his perceptions.

He adopts more realistic goals for himself.

He behaves in a more mature fashion.

He changes his maladjustive behaviors, even such a long-established one as chronic alcoholism.

He becomes more acceptant of others.

He becomes more open to the evidence, both to what is going on outside of himself, and to what is going on inside of himself.

He changes in his basic personality characteristics, in constructive ways.*

I think perhaps this is sufficient to indicate that these are learnings which are significant, which do make a difference.

Significant Learning in Education

I believe I am accurate in saying that educators too are interested in learnings which make a difference. Simple knowledge of facts has its value. To know who won the battle of Poltava, or when the umpteenth opus of Mozart was first performed, may win $64,000 or some other sum for the possessor of this information, but I believe educators in general are a little embarrassed by the assumption that the acquisition of such knowledge constitutes education. Speaking of this reminds me of a forceful statment made by a professor of agronomy in my freshman year in college. Whatever knowledge I gained in his course has departed completely, but I remember how, with World War I as his background, he was comparing factual knowledge with ammunition. He wound up his little discourse with the exhortation "Don't be a damned ammunition wagon; be a rifle!" I

---

*For evidence supporting these statements see references (7) and (9).

believe most educators would share this sentiment that knowledge exists primarily for use.

To the extent then that educators are interested in learnings which are functional, which make a difference, which pervade the person and his actions, then they might well look to the field of psychotherapy for leads or ideas. Some adaptation for education of the learning process which takes place in psychotherapy seems like a promising possiblity.

The Conditions of Learning in Psychotherapy

Let us then see what is involved, essentially, in making possible the learning which occurs in therapy. I would like to spell out, as clearly as I can, the conditions which seem to be present when this phenomenon occurs.

Facing a Problem

The client is, first of all, up against a situation which he perceives as a serious and meaningful problem. It may be that he finds himself behaving in ways in which he cannot control, or he is overwhelmed by confusions and conflicts, or his marriage is going on the rocks, or he finds himself unhappy in his work. He is, in short, faced with a problem with which he has tried to cope, and found himself unsuccessful. He is therefore eager to learn, even though at the same time he is frightened that what he discovers in himself may be disturbing. Thus one of the conditions nearly always present is an uncertain and ambivalent desire to learn or to change, growing out of a perceived difficulty in meeting life.

What are the conditions which this individual meets when he comes to a therapist? I have recently formulated a theoretical picture of the necessary and sufficient conditions which the therapist provides, if constructive change or significant learning is to occur (8). This theory is currently being tested in several of its aspects by empirical research, but it must still be regarded as theory based upon clincial experience rather than proven fact. Let me describe briefly the conditions which it seems essential that the therapist should provide.

Congruence

If therapy is to occur, it seems necessary that the therapist be, in the relationship, a unified, or integrated, or congruent person. What I mean is that within the relationship he is exactly what he *is*—not a façade, or a role, or a pretense. I have used the term "congruence" to refer to this accurate matching of experience with awareness. It is when the therapist is fully and accurately aware of what he is experiencing at this moment in the relationship, that he is fully congruent. Unless this congruence is present to a considerable degree it is unlikely that significant learning can occur.

Though this concept of congruence is actually a complex one, I believe all of us recognize it in an intuitive and commonsense way in individuals with whom we deal. With one individual we recognize that he not only means exactly what he says, but that his deepest feelings also match what he is expressing. Thus whether he is angry or affectionate or ashamed or enthusiastic, we sense that he is the same at all levels—in what he is experiencing at an organismic level, in his awareness at the conscious level, and in his words and communications. We furthermore recognize that he is acceptant of his immediate feelings. We say of such a person that we know "exactly where he stands." We tend to feel comfortable and secure in such a relationship. With another person we recognize that what he is saying is almost certainly a front or a façade. We wonder what he *really* feels, what he is really experiencing, behind this façade. We may also wonder if *he* knows what he really feels, recognizing that he may be quite unaware of the feelings he is actually experiencing. With such a person we tend to be cautious and wary. It is not the kind of relationship in which defenses can be dropped or in which significant learning and change can occur.

Thus this second condition for therapy is that the therapist is characterized by a considerable degree of congruence in the relationship. He is freely, deeply, and acceptantly himself, with his actual experience of his feelings and reactions matched by an accurate awareness of these feelings and reactions as they occur and as they change.

Unconditional Positive Regard

A third condition is that the therapist experiences a warm caring for the client—a caring which is not possessive, which demands no personal gratification. It is an atmosphere which simply demonstrates "I care"; not "I care for you *if* you behave thus and so." Standal (11) has termed this attitude "unconditional positive regard," since it has no conditions of worth attached to it. I have often used the term "acceptance" to describe this aspect of the therapeutic climate. It involves as much feeling of acceptance for the client's expression of negative, "bad," painful, fearful, and abnormal feelings as for his expression of "good," positive, mature, confident and social feelings. It involves an acceptance of and a caring for the client as a *separate* person, with permission for him to have his own feelings and experiences, and to find his own meanings in them. To the degree that the therapist can provide this safety-creating climate of unconditional positive regard, significant learning is likely to take place.

An Empathic Understanding

The fourth condition for therapy is that the therapist is experiencing an accurate, empathic understanding of the client's world as seen from the inside. To sense the client's private world as if it were your own, but without ever losing the "as if" quality—this is empathy, fear, or confusion as if it were your own, yet without your own anger, fear, or confusion getting bound up in it, is the condition we are endeavoring to describe. When the client's world is this clear to the therapist, and he moves about in it freely, then he can both communicate his understanding of what is clearly known to the client and can also voice meanings in the client's experience of which the client is scarcely aware. That such penetrating empathy is important for therapy is indicated by Fiedler's research in which items such as the following placed high in the description of relationships created by experienced therapists:

The therapist is well able to understand the patient's feelings.

The therapist is never in any doubt about what the patient means.

The therapist's remarks fit in just right with the patient's mood and content.

The therapist's tone of voice conveys the complete ability to share the patient's feelings. (3)

Fifth Condition

A fifth condition for significant learning in therapy is that the client should experience or perceive something of the therapist's congruence, acceptance, and empathy. It is not enough that these conditions exist in the therapist. They must, to some degree, have been successfully communicated to the client.

The Process of Learning in Therapy

It has been our experience that when these five conditions exist, a process of change inevitably occurs. The client's rigid perceptions of himself and of others loosen and become open to reality. The rigid ways in which he has construed the meaning of his experience are looked at, and he finds himself questioning many of the "facts" of his life, discovering that they are only "facts" because he has regarded them so. He discovers feelings of which he has been unaware, and experiences them, often vividly, in the therapeutic relationship. Thus he learns to be more open to all of his experience— the evidence within himself as well as the evidence without. He learns to *be* more of his experience—to be the feelings of which he has been frightened as well as the feelings he has regarded as more acceptable. He becomes a more fluid, changing, learning person.

The Mainspring of Change

In this process it is not necessary for the therapist to "motivate" the client or to supply the energy which brings about the change. Nor, in some sense, is the motivation supplied by the client, at least in any conscious way. Let us say rather that the motivation for learning and change springs from the self-actualizing tendency of life itself, the tendency for the organism to flow into all the differentiated channels of potential development, insofar as these are experienced as enhancing.

I could go on at very considerable length on this, but it is not my purpose to focus on the process of therapy and the learnings which take place, nor on the motivation for these learnings, but rather on the conditions which make them possible. So I will simply conclude this description of therapy by saying that it is a type of significant learning which takes place when five conditions are met:

When the client perceives himself as faced by a serious and meaningful problem;

When the therapist is a congruent person in the relationship, able to *be* the person he *is;*

When the therapist feels an unconditional positive regard for the client;

When the therapist experiences an accurate empathic understanding of the client's private world, and communicates this;

When the client to some degree experiences the therapist's congruence, acceptance, and empathy.

Implications for Education

What do these conditions mean if applied to education? Undoubtedly the teacher will be able to give a better answer than I out of his own experience, but I will at least suggest some of the implications.

Contact with Problems

In the first place it means that significant learning occurs more readily in relation to situations perceived as problems. I believe I have observed evidence to support this. In my own varying attempts to conduct courses and groups in ways consistent with my therapeutic experience, I have found such an approach more effective, I believe, in workshops than in regular courses, in extension courses than in campus courses. Individuals who come to workshops or extension courses are those who are in contact with problems which they recognize as problems. The student in the regular university course, and particularly in the required course, is apt to view the course as an experience in which he expects to remain passive or resentful or both, an experience which he certainly does not often see as relevant to his own problems.

Yet it has also been my experience that when a regular university class does perceive the course as an experience they can use to resolve problems which *are* of concern to them, the sense of release, and the thrust of forward movement is astonishing. And this is true of courses as diverse as Mathematics and Personality.

I believe the current situation in Russian education also supplies evidence on this point. When a whole nation perceives itself as being faced with the urgent problem of being behind—in agriculture, in industrial production, in scientific development, in weapons development—then an astonishing amount of significant learning takes place, of which the Sputniks are but one observable example.

So the first implication for education might well be that we permit the student, at any level, to be in real contact with the relevant problems of his existence, so that he perceives problems and issues which he wishes to resolve. I am quite aware that this implication, like the others I shall mention, runs sharply contrary to the current trends in our culture, but I shall comment on that later.

I believe it would be quite clear from my description of therapy that an overall implication for education would be that the task of the teacher is to create a facilitating classroom climate in which significant learning can take place. This general implication can be broken down into several sub-sections.

The Teacher's Real-ness

Learning will be facilitated, it would seem if the teacher is congruent. This involves the teacher's being the person that he is, and being openly aware of the attitudes he holds. It means that he feels acceptant toward his own real feelings. Thus he becomes a real person in the relationship with his students. He can be enthusiastic about subjects he likes, and bored by topics he does not like. He can be angry, but he can also be sensitive or sympathetic. Because he accepts his feelings as *his* feelings, he has no need to impose them on his students, or to insist that they feel the same way. He is a *person*, not a faceless embodiment of a curricular requirement, or a sterile pipe through which knowledge is passed from one generation to the next.

I can suggest only one bit of evidence which might support this view. As I think back over a number of teachers who have facilitated my own learning, it seems to me each one has this quality of being a real person. I wonder if your memory is the same. If so, perhaps it is less important that a teacher cover the allotted amount of the curriculum, or use the most approved audio-visual devices, than that he be congruent, real, in his relation to his students.

Acceptance and Understanding

Another implication for the teacher is that significant learning may take place if the teacher can accept the student as he is, and can understand the feelings he possesses. Taking the third and fourth conditions of therapy as specified above, the teacher who can warmly accept, who can provide an unconditional positive regard, and who can empathize with the feelings of fear, anticipation, and discouragement which are involved in meeting new material, will have done a great deal toward setting the conditions for learning. Clark Moustakas, in his book, *The Teacher and the Child* (5), has given many excellent examples of individual and group situations from kindergarten to high school, in which the teacher has worked toward just this type of goal. It will perhaps disturb some that when the teacher holds such attitudes, when he is willing to be acceptant of feelings, it is not only attitudes toward school work itself which are expressed, but feelings about parents, feelings of hatred for brother or sister, feelings of concern about self—the whole gamut of attitudes. Do such feelings have a right to exist openly in a school setting? It is my thesis that they do. They are related to the person's becoming, to his effective learning and effective functioning, and to deal understandingly and acceptantly with such feelings has a definite relationship to the learning of long division or the geography of Pakistan.

Provision of Resources

This brings me to another implication which therapy holds for education. In therapy the resources for learning one's self lie within. There is very little data which the therapist can supply which will be of help since the data to be dealt with exist within the person. In education this is not true. There are many resources of knowledge, of techniques, of theory, which constitute raw material for use. It seems to me that what I have said about therapy suggests that these materials, these resources, be made available to the students, not forced upon them. Here a wide range of ingenuity and sensitivity is an asset.

I do not need to list the usual resources which come to mind—books, maps, workbooks, materials, recordings, work-space, tools, and the like. Let me focus for a moment on the way the teacher uses himself and his knowledge and experience as a resource. If the teacher holds the point of view I have been expressing then he would probably want to make himself available to his class in at least the following ways:

He would want to let them know of special experience and knowledge he has in the field, and to let them know they could call on this knowledge. Yet he would not want them to feel that they must use him in this way.

He would want them to know that his own way of thinking about the field, and of organizing it, was available to them, even in lecture form, if they wished. Yet again he would want this to be perceived as an offer, which could as readily be refused as accepted.

He would want to make himself known as a resource-finder. Whatever might be seriously wanted by an individual or by the whole group to promote their learning, he would be very willing to consider the possibilities of obtaining such a resource.

He would want the quality of his relationship to the group to be such that his feelings could be freely available to them, without being imposed on them or becoming a restrictive influence on them. He thus could share the excitements and enthusiasms of his own learnings, without insisting that the students follow in his footsteps; the feelings of disinterest, satisfaction, bafflement, or pleasure which he feels toward individual or group activities, without this becoming either a carrot or a stick for the student. His hope would be that he could say, simply for himself, "I don't like that," and that the student with equal freedom could say, "But I do."

Thus whatever the resource he supplies—a book, space to work, a new tool, an opportunity for observation of an industrial process, a lecture based on his own study, a picture, graph or map, his own emotional reactions—he would feel that these were, and would hope they would be perceived as, offerings to be used if they were useful to the student. He would not feel them to be guides, or expectations, or commands, or impositions or requirements. He would offer himself, and all the other resources he could discover, for use.

The Basic Motive

It should be clear from this that his basic reliance would be upon the self-actualizing tendency in his students. The hypothesis upon which he would build is that students who are in real contact with life problems wish to learn, want to grow, seek to find out, hope to master, desire to create. He would see his function as that of developing such a personal relationship with his students, and such a climate in his classroom, that these natural tendencies could come to their fruition.

Some Omissions

These I see as some of the things which are implied by a therapeutic viewpoint for the educational process. To make them a bit sharper, let me point out some of the things which are not implied.

I have not included lectures, talks, or expositions of subject matter which are imposed on the students. All of these procedures might be a part of the experience if they were desired, explicitly or implicitly, by the students. Yet even here, a teacher whose work was following through a hypothesis based on therapy would be quick to sense a shift in that desire. He might have been requested to lecture to the group (and to give a *requested* lecture is *very* different from the usual classroom experience), but if he detected a growing disinterest and boredom, he would respond to that, trying to understand the feeling which has arisen in the group, since his response to their feelings and attitudes would take precedence over his interest in expounding material.

I have not included any program of evaluation of the student's learnings in terms of external criteria. I have not, in other words, included examinations. I believe that the testing of the student's achievements in order to see if he meets some criterion held by the teacher, is directly contrary to the implications of therapy for significant learning. In therapy, the examinations are set by *life*. The client meets them, sometimes passing, sometimes failing. He finds that he can use the resources of the therapeutic relationship and his experience in it to organize himself so that he can meet life's tests more satisfyingly next time. I see this as the paradigm for education also. Let me try to spell out a fantasy of what it would mean.

In such an education, the requirements for many life situations would be a part of the resources the teacher provides. The student would have available the knowledge that he cannot enter engineering school without so much math; that he cannot get a job in X corporation unless he has a college diploma; that he cannot become a psychologist without doing an independent doctoral research; that he cannot be a doctor without knowledge of chemistry; that he cannot even drive a car without passing an examination on rules of the road. These are requirements set, not by the teacher, but by life. The teacher is there to provide the resources which the student can use to learn so as to be able to meet these tests.

There would be other in-school evaluations of similar sort. The student might be faced with the fact that he cannot join the Math Club until he makes a certain score on a standardized mathematics test; that he cannot develop his camera film until he has shown an adequate knowledge of chemistry and lab techniques; that he cannot join the special literature section until he has shown evidence of both wide reading and creative writing. The natural place of evaluation in life is as a ticket of entrance, not as a club over the recalcitrant. Our experience in therapy would suggest that it should be the same way in the school. It would leave the student as a self-respecting, self-motivated person, free to choose whether he wished to put forth the effort to gain these tickets of entrance. It would thus refrain from forcing him into conformity, from sacrificing his creativity, and from causing him to live his life in terms of the standards of others.

I am quite aware that the two elements of which I have just been speaking—the lectures and expositions imposed by the teacher on the group, and the evaluation of the individual by the teacher, constitute the two major ingredients of current education. So when I say that experience in psychotherapy would suggest that they both be omitted, it should be quite clear that the implications of psychotherapy for education are startling indeed.

Probable Outcomes

If we are to consider such drastic changes as I have outlined, what would be the results which would justify them? There have been some research investigations of the outcomes of a student-centered type of teaching (1, 2, 4), though these studies are far from adequate. For one thing, the situations studied vary greatly in the extent to which they meet the conditions I have described. Most of them have extended only over a period of a few months, though one recent study with lower class children extended over a full year (4). Some involve the use of adequate controls, some do not.

I think we may say that these studies indicate that in classroom situations which at least attempt to approximate the climate I have described, the findings are as follows: Factual and curricular learning is roughly equal to the learning in conventional classes. Some studies report slightly more, some slightly less. The student-centered group shows gains significantly greater than the conventional class in personal adjustment, in self-initiated extra-curricular learning, in creativity, in self-responsibility.

I have come to realize, as I have considered these studies, and puzzled over the design of better studies which should be more informative and conclusive, that findings from such research will never answer our questions. For all such findings must be evaluated in terms of the goals we have for education. If we value primarily the learning of knowledge, then we may discard the conditions I have described as useless, since there is no evidence that they lead to a greater rate or amount of factual knowledge. We may then favor such measures as the one which I understand is advocated by a number of members of Congress—the setting up of a training school for scientists, modeled upon the military academies. But if we value creativity, if we deplore the fact that all of our germinal ideas in atomic physics, in psychology, and in other sciences have been borrowed from Europe, then we may wish to give a trial to ways of facilitating learning which give more promise of freeing the mind. If we value independence, if we are disturbed by the growing conformity of knowledge, of values, of attitudes, which our present system induces, then we may wish to set up conditions of learning which make for uniqueness, for self-direction, and for self-initiated learning.

Some Concluding Issues

I have tried to sketch the kind of education which would be implied by what we have learned in the field of psychotherapy. I have endeavored to suggest very briefly what it would mean if the central focus of the teacher's effort were to develop a relationship, an atmosphere, which was conducive to self-motivated, self-actualizing, significant learning. But this is a direction which leads sharply away from current educational practices and educational trends. Let me mention a few of the very diverse issues and questions which need to be faced if we are to think constructively about such an approach.

In the first place, how do we conceive the goals of education? The approach I have outlined has, I believe, advantages for achieving certain goals, but not for achieving others. We need to be clear as to the way we see the purposes of education.

What are the actual outcomes of the kind of education I have described? We need a great deal more of rigorous, hard-headed research to know the actual results of this kind of education as compared with conventional education. Then we can choose on the basis of the facts.

Even if we were to try such an approach to the facilitation of learning, there are many difficult issues. Could we possibly permit students to come in contact with real issues? Our whole culture—through the efforts of labor unions and management, through the attitudes of parents and teachers—is deeply committed to keeping young people away from any touch with real problems. They are not to work, they should not carry responsibility, they have no business in civic or political problems, they have no place in international concerns, they simply should be guarded from any direct contact with the real problems of individual and group living. They are not expected to help about the home, to earn a living, to contribute to science, to deal with moral issues. This is a deep seated trend which has lasted for more than a generation. Could it possibly be reversed?

Another issue is whether we could permit knowledge to be organized in and by the individual, or whether it is to be organized *for* the individual. Here teachers and educators line up with parents and national leaders to insist that the pupil must be guided. He must be inducted into knowledge we have organized for him. He cannot be trusted to organize knowledge in functional terms for himself. As Herbert Hoover says of high school students, "You simply cannot expect kids of those ages to determine the sort of education they need unless they have some guidance."* This seems so obvious to most people that even to question it is to seem somewhat unbalanced. Even a chancellor of a university questions whether freedom is really necessary in education, saying that perhaps we have overestimated its value. He says the Russians have advanced mightily in science without it, and implies that we should learn from them.

Still another issue is whether we would wish to oppose the strong current trend toward education as drill in factual knowledge. All must learn the same facts in the same way. Admiral Rickover states it as his belief that "in some fashion we must devise a way to introduce uniform standards into American education. . . . For the first time, parents would have a real yardstick to measure their schools. If the local school continued to teach such pleasant subjects as "life adjustment' . . . instead of French and physics, its diploma would be, for all the world to see, inferior."† This is a statement of a very prevalent view. Even such a friend of forward looking views in education as Max Lerner says at one point, "All that a school can ever hope to do is to equip the student with tools which he can later use to become an educated man" (5, p. 741). It is quite clear that he despairs of significant learning taking place in our school system, and feels that it must take place outside. All the school can do is to pound in the tools.

One of the most painless ways of inculcating such factual tool knowledge is the "teaching machine" being devised by B.F. Skinner and his associates (10). This group is demonstrating that the teacher is an outmoded and ineffective instrument for teaching arithmetic, trigonometry, French, literary appreciation, geography, or other factual subjects. There is simply no doubt in my mind that these teaching machines, providing immediate rewards for "right" answers, will be further developed, and will come into wide use. Here is a new contribution from the field of the behavioral sciences with which we must come to terms. Does it take the

Time, December 2, 1957.
†*Ibid.*

place of the approach I have described, or is it supplemental to it? Here is one of the problems we must consider as we face toward the future.

I hope that by posing these issues, I have made it clear that the double-barreled question of what constitutes significant learning, and how it is to be achieved, poses deep and serious problems for all of us. It is not a time when timid answers will suffice. I have tried to give a definition of significant learning as it appears in psychotherapy, and a description of the conditions which facilitate such learning. I have tried to indicate some implications of these conditions for education. I have, in other words, proposed one answer to these questions. Perhaps we can use what I have said, against the twin backdrops of current public opinion and current knowledge in the behavioral sciences, as a start for discovering some fresh answers of our own.

References

1. Faw, Volney. A psychotherapeutic method of teaching psychology". *Amer. Psychol.* 4: 104-09, 1949.
2. Faw, Volney, "Evaluation of student-centered teaching." Unpublished manuscript, 1954.
3. Fiedler, F.E. "A comparison of therapeutic relationships in psychoanalytic, non-directive and Adlerian therapy". *J. Consult. Psychol.* 1950, 14, 436-45.
4. Jackson, John H. "The relationship between psychological climate and the quality of learning outcomes among lower-status pupils". Unpublished Ph.D. thesis, University of Chicago, 1957.
5. Lerner, Max. *America as a Civilization.* New York: Simon & Schuster, 1957.
6. Moustakas, Clark. *The Teacher and the Child.* New York: McGraw-Hill, 1956.
7. Rogers, C.R. *Client-Centered Therapy.* Boston: Houghton Mifflin Co., 1951.
8. Rogers, C.R. "The necessary and sufficient conditions of therapeutic personality change.". *J. Consult. Psychol.* 1957, 21, 95-103.
9. Rogers, C.R., and R. Dymond, (eds.). *Psychotherapy and Personality Change.* University of Chicago Press, 1954.
10. Skinner, B.F. "The Science of learning and the art of teaching". *Harvard Educational Review* 1954, 24, 86-97.
11. Standal, Stanley. "The need for positive regard: A contribution to client-centered theory". Unpublished Ph.D. thesis, University of Chicago, 1954.

9. Confrontation and Encounter

Clark E. Moustakas

Every person desires to have a life of meaning and authenticity. What value is activity if it lacks meaning? What significance is work without love? What is fulfillment in the absence of a dream? What is achievement without the spontaneous excitement of a wondering learner? What is life without companionship?

Every individual wishes to take his stand in relation. To be with another person in a fundamental sense sustains and nourishes us to our own fulfillment. The place where one lives and works, whether it be home or clinic or classroom, is a sanctuary where roots are formed between persons, and where almost perceptible emergence of self occurs. Every year, each day, each moment with another human being must count. Otherwise life is foolish and ugly and wrong. To employ one's resources and talents and skills in false, unethical or destructive means is an utterly wasteful and empty existence.

What meaning can rules and roles and doctrines and concepts have when persons live together in a deeply human sense? To care for another person, to accept him as he is, to love him in his own ways, these are living encounters which enable a person to realize a growing selfhood.

We all know the meaning of compassion. Each of us has witnessed the child, alone and friendless, searching for eyes which embrace, seeking a smile which includes, looking for a gesture which affirms. Each of us has experienced despair, loneliness, personal anguish, inner conflicts. When we are in trouble, only the caring of another person gives us courage and strength to face the unknown, to talk of our pain and suffering, to express our guilt, shame, humiliation, to be released from sorrow in such a way that we keep our integrity while divulging our trespasses and sins.

Each of us seeks fellowship and a place where freedom and affection abide as lively human dimensions. Each of us wishes intimate and profound associations with others, a friend who will love us no matter what we do or say. Each of us wants to make our brief days on earth an ever new vision and intensity of beauty and truth, to make our existence worthy of being human and being alive. And each and every one of us counts no matter where or who we are. Each of us is entirely unique, known only briefly in our truest reality, yet within these brief encounters, solidarity and courage and discovery emerge.

Significant, enduring meanings, living thoughts and feelings can be created in the classroom in genuine confrontations and encounters without in any way limiting academic growth or achievement. The confrontation is a meeting of persons involving an issue or dispute. Conflicts arise and feelings grow between persons until they no longer can bear to live with each other. The confrontation happens sometimes suddenly and unexpectedly but always unpredictably. It requires that individuals remain together until there is a resolution of feeling. It may last a short while or a long time depending on the requirements of the situation. The individuals may terminate the confrontation, still at odds as far as the issue is concerned, but not at odds with each other. This is the important point for the classroom teacher to realize—the child must be free to maintain his own identity. He must be respected as he is, with his own concepts and perceptions however wrong they may appear to the teacher. He must be accepted in his own ways. In the classroom confrontation, the child must have the right to be in disagreement with his teacher, even when the dispute ends. And paradoxical as this appears, only when the persons can end in disagreement, if this is the reality of their experience, it is possible for them to feel better, be free of tension, and establish genuine bonds. When the teacher forces the child through repetition, conditioning, belittling, through group pressure, or in other ways uses subtle, brainwashing devices, when the teacher cuts the child off or beats him down, the child soon realizes the only acceptable way is the path of conformity, the taking on of the words and ways of the one in authority. Increasingly the child becomes insensitive to his own self and unresponsive to his own experience. He can become numb to criticism and rebuke, develop a suspicious or mechanical approach against further attacks and come to be unfeeling in his associations with others.

Recently I visited a second-grade classroom. When the children saw the principal and I enter the room, they were all eager to read for us. The teacher asked for volunteers. A child, with a smiling face and shining eyes, sitting next to me, is called to read. I hear her sigh of joy as she begins, "Casey Joins the Circus." Apparently, she has learned that a good reader varies his tone of voice, reads loud enough for others to hear and reads fluently. Wanting to make an impression, wanting to get the praise of her teacher and classmates, she hurries through the paragraph assigned to her. But something is wrong. In the middle of her reading, Mrs. Bell interrupts the child. She pushes the book away from the child's face and says in a firm voice, hovering over the child, "You are reading carelessly. That's not showing respect for what is printed on the page. It's not showing respect for our visitors or the other boys and girls. You are making sense but you simply are not reading the words in the book. I've told you about this before, Betsy. Now you go back and read what's printed there so we can all follow you." The child returns to the begining of the paragraph, but something has happened. She has no direct, open way of responding. The accusing, staring faces of the other children frighten her. She reads in a reluctant manner, pronounces words haltingly. There is a weak, muffled quality in her voice. She has been hurt. Inside I feel her tears. She is no longer certain. She completes the reading and slumps wearily into her chair. She does not volunteer again that morning.

The real tragedy is not in the critical words of the teacher or in the subdued, minimized child, but in the fact that no relationship exists. There is the teacher as law-giver and statement-maker, as the one in authority. There is a voice, belittling, shaming, minimizing, humiliating the child into exact reading. The teacher uses every available resource, the visitors, other children, herself, the book, to prove her point and impress the child. And it's all done matter-of-factly, as professional duty. It is all so unconditional, pure, impersonal, feelingless. Then there is the subdued, frightened, muffled, crawling voice of the child. The child reads and she reads and she reads, every word in the lesson. Now I ask you, is it worth killing that spontaneity, that joy, that wonder in a little girl's voice as she tried to please her audience, for the sake of a word-by-word conformity to the printed page!

This girl is not just a reader, not merely a machine producing and transmitting sound. There beside me is a human being. She is really there, wanting so much to see her teacher smile, a smile which tells her all is right in the world, a glance which helps her to feel she is valued, even when she makes mistakes. This teacher is not a person. She is performing a function. She confronts the child with her inadequacies but the confrontation never gets off the ground, never rises from below, never gets beyond the initial reproof. Oh, yes, the child goes through the motion of reading, but she is no longer there. She cannot face her teacher any more.

No teacher is perfect. We all make mistakes. But to commit a wrong, to lower the dignity of a child and not be aware that that dignity has been impaired, is much more serious than the child's skipping of words during oral reading. The real tragedy is the teacher's lack of sensitivity and her failure to recognize the child as a person.

In a true confrontation the persons always remain alive. And because there is awareness and knowledge and sensitivity, the skirmish, the battle, the argument, the fact-to-fact struggle takes its natural course and opens new pathways of relatedness between persons.

But when a teacher loses sight of the child as a human being, when she fails to gather in the child's presence as a person, there is no reality between them, there is no relationship. There is no mutuality.

And this is what happens in many classroom confrontations, in many situations where potential growth exists between persons. The persons are lost. The discrepancy or issue becomes all that matters. And the loudest voice, the strongest figure, the person in authority carries out his office of command. Gradually the child is forced into a process of desensitization where feelings and senses are muffled and subdued until eventually he is no longer aware that he is not experiencing from within. When people reject, humiliate, hurt, belittle, control, dominate, and brutalize others, without any awareness of what they are doing, when there is no concern on the part of others for what is being done to them, there is extreme danger that man will cease to be man, that whatever is human will be permanently impaired or so significantly reduced that the life of man will be as automatic as a self-moving machine and as mechanical as counting beads on an abacus.

Go into any school. Notice the difference in climate in the kindergarten and sixth grade. The very young children are in touch with themselves. Their feelings correspond with their actions. They are open and direct. One feels welcomed, gathered-in in their presence. In contrast, the sixth graders are more devious, indirect, calculating. Too much that is meaningful and real in their experience remains latent and undisclosed.

Desensitization occurs through a process of deprivation and separation where one is treated as an object, where skills and subject matter are more significant than learners, where goals must be pursued regardless of the real wishes, aspirations and capacities of persons, where rationalizing, explaining, and analyzing take place of spontaneity, humanistic experience and natural feeling. When the teacher's role is to observe and direct, when the teacher notes the child, probes him, writes him up, and breaks him down into specific traits, weaknesses, and strengths, she treats the child as an object for study and academic nourishment, when the teacher is concerned with techniques to the exclusion of the unique and varying differences in individuals, the child loses touch with his own senses, his own identity. He builds a wall around him to protect himself. He becomes insensitive to laughter and mimicry and sarcasm. In its extreme form, what happens in everyday life toward dehumanization is not unlike what occured in death camps during World War II. The dehumanization of the prisoner of war is forcefully described by Viktor Frankl (7, 19-20) in this brief narrative of his experiences in four concentration camps:

"At first the prisoner looked away if he saw the punishment parades of another group; he could not bear to see fellow prisoners march up and down for hours in the mire, their movements directed by blows. Days or weeks later things changed. The prisoner did not avert his eyes any more. By then his feelings were blunted, and he watched unmoved. He stood unmoved while a twelve-year-old boy was carried in who had been forced to stand at attention for hours in the snow or to work outside with bare feet because there were no shoes for him in the camp. His toes had become frostbitten, and the doctor on duty picked off the black gangrenous stumps with tweezers, one by one. Disgust, horror, and pity are emotions that our spectator could not really feel any more. The sufferers, the dying and the dead, became such commonplace sights to him after a few weeks of camp life that they could not move him any more."

The current rise of existentialism and Zen Buddhism, both of which are concerned with the unique, humanness of the person living in the world, grows out of the dangers in conformity and dehumanization. Norman Cousins (6) has registered this editorial warning:

"What is happening, I believe, is that the natural reactions of the individual against violence are being blunted. The individual is being desensitized by living history. He is developing new reflexes and new responses that tend to slow up the moral imagination and relieve him of essential indignation over impersonal hurt. He is becoming casual about brutality. He makes his adjustments to the commonplace, and nothing is more commonplace in our age than the ease with which life can be smashed or shattered. The range of the violence sweeps from the personal to the impersonal, from the amusements of the crowd to the policies of nations. It is in the air, quite literally. It has lost the sting of surprise.

"The desensitization of twentieth-century man is more than a danger to the common safety. It represents the loss or impairment of the noblest faculty of human life—the ability to be aware both of suffering and beauty; the ability to share sorrow and create hope; the ability to think and respond beyond one's wants. There are some things we have no right ever to get used to. One of these most certainly is brutality. The other is the irrational. Both brutality and the irrational have now come together and are moving towards a dominant pattern. If the pattern is to be resisted and changed, a special effort must be made. A very special effort."

In contrast to the confrontation which does not get beyond the initial criticism, is the confrontation in which the teacher exposes the child to his misdemeanor but remains with him and enables him to come to terms with his own immorality, wrong-doing, or irresponsibility. In the true confrontation, the relationship unfolds into more and more meaningful expressions of the self, release of feelings, and resolution of issues and conflicts toward growing insights, and awarenesses, and toward a sense of responsibility. In such a confrontation, the teacher is all there, fully committed as a person. It is sheer nonsense to consider whether, in the moments of the full human exertion of a confrontation, the teacher can adapt himself to the role of educator or therapist or disciplinarian. The teacher is there as a total person engaged in a meeting in which all dimensions and resources of self converge, in which the whole being comes to grips with an impelling human conflict.

Within the experience of confronting another with angry or hostile criticism, there is the promise of a bond of friendship, of significant roots being established within the relationship. The confrontation is a way to deeper intimacy and relatedness, to an authentic life between persons, but the teacher must maintain a living awareness of his feelings and must be honest enough and courageous enough to let the initial breach heal through the silent, sacred, covenant of love and strong enough to maintain the human sense whatever else may be cancelled out in the issue or dispute.

A Cluster of Grapes (1)

A confrontation which resulted in the education of character is illustrated in "A Cluster of Grapes," an autobiographical story of Takeo Arishima, recently translated by Kazuko Yoshinaga. This is the story of the painful shame a child experienced in facing his beloved teacher with his dishonesty. Takeo relates this memorable experience from his childhood:

"I was fond of drawing pictures in my childhood. My school was located in Yamanote in Yokohama where most children and the teachers were western people. On my way home from school, I saw warships and merchant ships staying in the raw on the deep blue sea. From some of the chimneys, smoke was coming out. I used to stand on the shore and watch the scene. I tried to draw it on paper. However, the colors of the clear deep blue sea and the crimson lines of the boats, I could not make right with the paints I had—no matter how many times I tried.

"Suddenly I remembered the imported paints which my friend had at school. He was a western boy and two years older than I. His name was Jim. Jim's paints were in a light wooden box. All his paints were pretty but particularly his deep blue and crimson paints were beautiful. If only I had his paints! I would paint the sea-scene as nearly as a real one. From that day, I became more and more anxious to have those two beautiful paints for my own. I was a coward. I could not ask my mother nor my father to buy the paints. Every day this was the thought in my heart.

"We ate lunch with our teacher; even this pleasant time I could not enjoy. My heart was restless. My heart was a dark contrast to the brilliant sun in the sky. If anyone recognized my face, it must have been faint and pale. I was constantly caught in the strong wish for those beautiful paints. I wanted them so much my heart ached. I turned my face to Jim softly wondering if he recognized my mind. Though I thought I saw suspicion in his eyes as he looked at me, I became more and more tempted to have his paints.

"One day, after lunch, while the other children went out to play, only I, at the bottom of my soul, stayed in the classroom. My eyes ran to Jim's desk. I thought: 'If I lift that lid I will find the box, the little square paints, the beautiful blue and crimson paints.' My heart beat terribly hard as if it would stop my breath. I was sitting quietly on my chair, but I was irritated and restless.

"The bell rang—the sign that recess was over. I could see the children going toward the washroom, laughing and talking. Half in a dream I went to Jim's table and lifted the lid of his desk. Quickly I opened the box, took out the two beautiful paints and shoved them into my pocket. Then I hurried into the line with the other children to wait for our teacher. I wanted very much to see Jim, how he looked, but I could not turn my head toward him. The words spoken by my teacher came to my ears but I did not hear. Now and then she looked at me with a puzzled expression. The hours passed. I felt everyone was watching me. It was time for recess again. The teacher left the room. The tallest boy in the class came over and shouted 'come out.' My heart beat wildly. I started shivering. I was taken to a corner of the playground. Voices yelled, 'You have Jim's paints, don't you?' 'Put them here.' Then Jim spoke, 'I had all my paints before recess. When I came back, I discovered two missing. You're the only one who stayed in the classroom.' The accusing faces stared at me. Hands pushed hard against me. From my pockets, they took a piece of marble, a cake of metal, cards, and *the two paints*. My body trembled and ached. My eyes darkened. I felt shamed, weakened in soul. I had done something I could never erase. This is the end, I thought. I began sobbing. Someone yelled in a despising, hateful voice, 'You can't frighten us by tears!'

"They grabbed hold of me and pushed me forward to my teacher's office. From inside a sweet voice rang out, 'Come in.' This was the most difficult moment in my life, to face my teacher in disgrace. Seeing us rush into the room she seemed surprised. 'What do you want?' she asked. The tallest boy told her in detail how I stole Jim's paints. She looked at me with a gentle face, asking 'Is it true?' It was terribly painful. I could not answer. I cried real deep. She spoke to the others, 'You may go to your classroom.' Then quietly she stood up. She held my shoulders into her arms and asked in a low voice, 'Did you return the paints?' I nodded affirmatively. She asked gently, 'Do you think your deed was desirable?' I bit my trembling lip again and again. I could not stop crying. From my eyes tears flowed. I wanted to die in my teachers arms. She spoke again, 'It's all right, if you understand well. For the next class you may remain here, on the couch.' Then the bell rang. She took her book from her desk. Looking at me, she picked a cluster of grapes from the vine just outside her window. She dropped the grapes on my lap and went out of the room. I became very sad and felt lonely, as I considered the wrong I had done my teacher. I could not eat the grapes. I sobbed continously until I fell asleep. I was wakened by a light touch on my shoulder. My teacher reassured me, 'You need not have such a sad face. Go home now and remember you must come tomorrow, no matter how you feel. If you do not come, I will be sad.' She slipped the grapes into my bag. I ate them on the way home.

"The next morning I did not feel like going to school. I tried hard wishing my stomach would hurt but not even one tooth ached. I walked very slowly and wandered toward school. It seemed to me I could not go through the school gate. I started to retrace my steps toward home but the vision of my teacher's face and sweet sad eyes pushed strong within me. I opened the gate and walked toward the school door.

"And then it happened. Jim flew to me. He took my hand. His face told me that the happenings of yesterday were in the past. He kindly pulled me to him and to our teacher's room. Our teacher opened the door. As we came into her room, she said, 'Jim, you understood. Now you will become good friends.' Jim pulled my hand lightly and shook hands with me. His face was radiant and smiling. I could never express my gratitude. I just smiled. The teacher had a happy face. She asked, 'Did you enjoy yesterday's grapes?' I answered, 'Yes!' She reached through the window and picked a cluster of grapes. Cutting it in half with a slender silver scissors, she handed a bunch to each of us. The beauty of her white hands and the purple grapes I remember vividly. Since then I have become a better person. Now when autumn comes, I remember the cluster of grapes, beautiful purple dotted with white, and all that they once meant to me."

Here is a totally different confrontation, a genuine opportunity for growth which was fully utilized. Here is a teacher who answers a child's theft with love. This teacher is concerned with the child as a person and recognizes that he is caught in a crisis of childhood. She lets him see that she continues to care for him even when he is in trouble, even when he commits a crime against his peers. Her devotion, her dedication, is always there, full, unqualified, steady, pure, unwavering. She lets the child see that whatever he does, however dishonest he might temporarily become, she will always be there as a trusting, loving, and believing person. And what could mean more to a human being in time of wrongdoing and irresponsibility, and sin, in time of failure, and disorder, and agitation, to know that another human being cares no matter what?

Inevitably, it hurts to be at odds with others, but the pain is inherent in the situation of wrongdoing or failure. It is not misery created and imposed from outside. The pain and anguish are healed through the understanding presence of another person. In the Cluster of Grapes, the teacher helped the child come to terms with his envy and dishonesty. Through facing the inner turmoil and pain, in the confrontation with a gentle, loving person, he came to realize firmness of character, courage to face himself, and a spirit of solidarity and fellowship which he had not known before with his classmates. The situation offered fruitful promise and the teacher entered into it and remained with it until positive emergence of self was realized. Without in any way lessening the guilt and humiliation the child felt, without in any way lessening the wrongfulness of the act or the child's sense of responsibility for his behavior, she helped him to expiate his sin, absolve his feeling of guilt and develop a strength of character. And long after the events of life in school left him he still remembered the delicate hand of his teacher, the cluster of grapes, and what these symbolized in the education of characters.

This is exactly what a true confrontation offers—an opportunity for the teacher to meet the child on a new and vital level, not just an argument or issue, not just the uncovering or discovering of a child's sins and misdemeanors, or his faults and shortcomings, but a face-to-face meeting, a center-to-center relatedness between two persons in which the controversy or exposure is only the beginning or the incident which gives rise to a direct facing of one's self in the presence of another person where a growing bond, a beautiful reality comes into existence and provides the basis for living with others in a fundamental growing sense. The confrontation offers the opportunity for a completely new understanding and awareness because it is not a routine exchange between individuals, or a series of habitual acts, or an unimaginative lesson in facts and skills. It is a real meeting, a real coming to grips with life in its fundamental meaning. It calls for a firm bracing to resist the tendency to devaluate and dehumanize. It is a real challenge to all of one's reserves. It means bringing strength where there is weakness, good where there is evil, truth where there is dishonesty, openness where there is restrictiveness, beauty where there is ugliness.

In the creative disputation, each person must be aware of the other's full legitimacy. Neither must lose sight of the fact that he is seeking in his own way, with whatever talents and skills he possesses, to find an authentic existence, to find some meaningful way to live, to express the truth as he sees it, with a strength of conviction. In no way is either person reduced by this. The essence of recognition is manifested in the creative confrontation where a living truth eventually arises and endures. In the classroom, the teacher has an additional challenge and responsibility. Without the action of the spirit being in any way weakened, the teacher must be over there with the wholly concrete spirit of this unique being who stands with him in the unique, living atmosphere of a classroom confrontation. Such a confrontation, within the healthy atmosphere of love and relatedness, has an educational value.

In his essay on the education of character, Buber (3, p. 107-108) forcefully describes the difficulty of creative resolution of conflict between teacher and child, as illustrated in this passage: "He must use his own insight wholeheartedly; he must not blunt the piercing impact of his knowledge, but he must at the same time have in readiness the healing ointment for the heart pierced by it. Not for a moment may he conduct a dialectical maneuver instead of the real battle for truth. But if he is the victor he has to help the vanquished endure defeat; and if he cannot conquer the self-willed soul that faces him (for victories over souls are not so easily won), then he has to find the word of love which alone can help to overcome so difficult a situation."

The teacher is sometimes afraid to confront a child who is hostile, caustic, or vengeful. Such a teacher avoids and avoids until the accumulation of feelings becomes so unbearable an explosion occurs. The teacher loses control. Once the self is out of control, there is no possibility to bring about a positive resolution of the problem. But when the hateful, rejecting emotions subside, there is always hope that the teacher can come to terms with the child and reach a depth of relatedness and mutuality. The threat of anxiety in facing an embittered, destructive child can be eliminated only in an actual confrontation with the dreaded child because until we actually meet him, we cannot know him. We cannot know whether we can live with him, whether we can face the issue or crisis and maintain our own identity with love.

Viewing the child solely as an immature learner is a way of escaping confronting him, thinking of him only as a student who is slow or lazy or careless or in any other external framework, are ways of avoiding the feelings which emerge in a controversial meeting. Considering him as the "other," or in whatever categories or rubrics, is all part of the estrangement which results when professional roles separate and alienate teacher and child as persons.

In the true confrontation, the external, objective framework is abandoned. The teacher departs from the embeddedness of the familiar and goes forth to an unknown meeting with the child. The threat of *acute* anxiety to some extent can be controlled by avoiding the unknown, by restricting the scope of life, by remaining in the embeddedness of the familiar and not venturing out. Because this makes for stagnation and constriction, the determination to go forward is always present to keeping open the doors to an expanding life (11, p. 45).

Brian

Brian had been coming for weekly therapy sessions for almost a year when his intense feelings of love and hate reached a peak. For three months, each experience had begun with a sword and gun battle between us. He screamed with delight each time he "pierced or cut" me, each time he shot and killed me. When these battles were first initiated we had agreed to keep them within a ten-minute time limit. Following the battle with me, he would proceed to shoot and kill all human and animal figures in the room. He would take a rifle and scrape to the floor all items on tables and the tops of cabinets. Often he would open the plastic paint containers and place them at the edge of a shelf. He would shoot at the containers until the paint sprayed against the walls and onto the floors. This barrage and hostile attack had been repeated in similar pattern for thirteen weeks. Then one day we faced each other on a different interpersonal level.

The usual ten-minute battle had been completed but Brian refused to stop. He decided to use me as a target for what he called "bow and arrow" practice. I explained that there were items in the room that he could use but that I would rather not be his target. The following conversation took place:

Mr. M: Brian, I have already explained I do not want to be used as a target. (As I express my feeling, Brian shoots again, this time hitting my arm.)

Mr. M: Brian, that hurt. Perhaps that's what you want . . . to hurt me. (Brian is about to shoot again.)

Mr. M: No Brian, I will not permit it again. I'm going to have to insist that you give me the bow and arrows. I do not intend to let you shoot me again. (Brian laughs nervously, with a sadistic glee in his voice. He tries to pull away but I hold the bow firmly. He drops the arrows.)

Mr. M: I'll just put these out of reach for the rest of this hour. You can play with them again next time you come. (Brian throws the bow at me. I pick it up and remove it. He picks up a pistol, gun belt, and knife and throws them at me with much force. I go over to him and hold his arms.)

Mr. M: I can see nothing will satisfy you until you've hurt me. You're determined to have it your way, but I'm just as determined not to be a target for your attacks. If you persist I'm going to have to make all these things out of bounds for the rest of the time. (Brian laughs in my face as I talk to him. He pulls away.)

Brian: You never let me do anything. All you ever think of is No! No! No!

Mr. M: Yes, I know. You think I stop you at every turn.

Brian: (Throws a container of paint at me.) I hate you.

Mr. M: You have every right to hate me but I will not permit you to throw things at me. For the rest of this time this entire section of the playroom is out of bounds. (Brian is infuriated. He glares angrily at me. His eyes focus on the blackboard, a cunning look crosses his face, and a sneering smile.)

Brian: Will you play tic-tac-toe with me?

Mr. M: Yes, if you'd like me to, but I saw your thought. I know what you intend doing. If you throw one more item at me I'm going to have to do something drastic. (The game begins. Suddenly Brian begins laughing wildly. He throws the chalk and eraser at me. He tries to run to the "out of bounds" area. I block his path. He picks up a pile of books and throws them.)

Mr. M: All right Brian. Everything in the room is out of bounds for the rest of the time. You may have only this small space here. We can sit and talk or just sit.

Brian: You can't make me stay in this part.

Mr. M: Oh, yes I can. We've reached a point now where this is the only place we have. (Pause)

Brian: I hate you. (Pause) I could kill you.

Mr. M: Yes, you really want to hurt me the way you feel I have hurt you. (Brian slaps me.)

Mr. M: I now must hold your arms. (Suddenly Brian completely relaxes. He lays his head on my shoulder.)

Brian: You never let the baby have his bottle.

Mr. M: You always had to cry and throw things before you were fed.

Brian: I want my bottle.

Mr. M: Would you like me to rock you? (Sitting together quietly on the floor, the therapist rocks Brian a few minutes. Brian becomes tense again.)

Brian: I hate you. I could kill you. (Brian begins spitting. I turn him around.)

Mr. M: It's as hard for me to have to hold you as it is for you to be held. I know you are doing what you feel you must, but we have reached a point now where I am doing what I feel I must. (Brian screams and laughs shrilly.)

Mr. M: It's time to leave now, Brian. Do you want to walk out by yourself or do you want me to take you out?

Brian: I'll go myself. (Brian walks toward the door. As he reaches it he picks up several items and throws them at me. He comes toward me and pushes and punches at me. I take him and pull him out the door.)

Mr. M: I realize, Brian, you couldn't hold to your decision. It's all right. (Brian begins to cry silently.)

Brian: I hate you and I never want to see you again.

Mr. M: But I want to see you again. I'll be here at the same time next week. (Brian leaves.)

This was a full, vital complete experience of two persons, involving much struggle, suffering, and pain, but also a definite growth experience. The limits were important not only because they provided a structure or form in which self-exploration could occur but also because they emerged within a situation where child and therapist faced each other as whole beings and lived through a significant controversy, forming deep ties between them and the roots of a healthy relationship.

The dispute over the broken limit significantly affected the nature of any experiences in psychotherapy. When Brian returned, he greeted me with a new feeling of intimacy and relatedness. He plunged into new areas of conflict and emotionalized expression. Having lived through a significant controversy with his therapist, having met his therapist as a person, Brian was able to verbalize his feelings of self-doubt, to say that his parents considered him a "bad," destructive child, and to relate directly a number of crucial experiences in which he had been severely denied as a self. Thus, in spite of the apparent breach, child and therapist formed deep ties between them which enabled the child to develop a sense of self and the freedom of real expression.

I conclude this section on confrontation with two illustrations. The first involves many direct issues between teacher and child with reference to the child's attacks on others and the second is a confrontation between a teacher and a group of children.

Richard and Mrs. King

I received Ricky in first grade with the fore-knowledge that as a kindergartener he had been able to antagonize and successfully fight several second and third graders. This gave him something of a personal standing, if not a social one, in the eyes of his class and his teacher. He was also introduced to the principal many times.

I discounted his infamous first year. I was not sure which child he was during the first few days of school but he set about enlightening me soon afterwards. Whenever there was an unusual amount of loud talking I would ask, "Who's shouting?" Ricky would answer, "It's me, Ricky Holway." After a few days of instruction I knew Ricky well. He was usually sliding, running, or galloping around the room. And he always kept his eyes on me while he created the furor. As soon as I looked up and noticed him, he stopped.

In straightening out names and learning who the children were, I found that I had two boys named Ricky. The children identified Ricky Holway as "the one who fights." I said that I hadn't seen any fighting so that wasn't going to help me to know the boys. Ricky said he would start a fight and then I would know. I laughed and told him that I'd remember now because he was the Ricky who had such a good sense of humor. He seemed to think this over, suspiciously.

In the beginning, I had asked the children to do a set of big and small drawings. Ricky was quick to point out that that was kindergarten work. He said loudly, "Aw, that's baby stuff. We did that in kindergarten." I answered lightly, "Of course it's kindergarten work. I want to be sure you can do it before we go on to reading and writing."

Ricky drew—all in purple, as I remember.

A few days later, our principal happened to come into our room. She exclaimed, "Oh, there's Ricky Holway. You're lucky to have him in your room because he's such a good worker.

Ricky slumped down in his chair and scowled. I let it pass. But later in the morning he was talking and teasing his neighbor instead of working on the assignment. I asked him to quiet down, addressing him, with sarcasm:

"I thought our principal said you were such a good worker."

I was sorry the moment I said it. His whole manner changed to one of belligerence, and he shouted.

"Aw, she's a liar! I ain't a good worker. And you know it and she knows it."

I walked over to his desk, leaned down, and said in a low voice,

"I will not permit you to call our principal a liar . . . nor anyone else. I think she was sincere in complimenting you because at the time you were one of the few people in the class who was working. She meant it. I'm sorry you didn't believe her."

Ricky thought that over and worked quietly the remainder of the day without comment.

The next day, while we were practicing writing names, Ricky asked for a new name tag. He said he wanted Richard on it, not Ricky. He said he didn't like the name Ricky any more. Besides, there was another Ricky in the class. Since he had previously shown a marked tendency to take short cuts in his work, I pointed out that Richard was longer and more difficult to write. He said, "That's all right, I want my own name." I made the tag for him. I thought he wrote his name very well and told him so. I have had good neat papers from him ever since. And from that day I called him Richard instead of Ricky.

Following the christening, for many days Richard finished his work so quickly that I asked to see his papers and then congratulated him on work well done. Someone announced that Richard was not finished because he had not made the drawing. I asked the others if they liked to draw. Everyone nodded, shouted in the affirmative. I told them that Richard did not like to draw just then but one day he might wish to. The class accepted this gracefully. All except Mike, who impishly asked,

"Is Richard your pet?"

Richard spun around to Mike and yelled,

"Do you want to fight?"

"No," answered Mike, "I'm littler than you."

Richard was the first to laugh and we all joined him.

In the early weeks of school, Richard occasionally would strike out at someone while we were on the playground. Whenever that happened I insisted he withdraw from the group. During games, children were quick to accuse Richard when they had been bumped or pushed. One day I told the class that if they played with Richard outside, they had to remember that he played a rougher game than most boys and that if they didn't want to take the chance of being hurt, perhaps they should play with someone else.

I can't tell you when, but sometime during the first six or eight weeks of school, Richard stopped hitting. I can recall no scrimmages on the playground during the past month and a half.

Richard has had a special privilege since the second week of school. That privilege of coming into the building and into the room as soon as he arrives at school. The reason for this is that he created chaos just standing in line before the bell. Three or more times a week a service girl would usher him in and report that he had been calling them names under his breath, but not so softly that his invectives could not be heard. When asked why, he said,

"Aw, they're bossy. They're always telling a guy what to do."

I pointed out to him that the service girls were out in the halls in the morning for an important reason, that they had to get up early to be there, and then to go across the street to another building to be on time for their own classes—no matter what the weather.

"Yeah, but they're still bossy," Richard insisted.

I said, "Sure they're bossy. Some more so than others. But they have a responsibility for helping children and seeing that safety rules are followed. Many people become bossy when gentler methods fail. How do you think you would act if you were on the service squad?"

Richard answered quickly, "I'd line 'em up against the wall and let 'em have it if kids gave me trouble."

"And aren't you lucky that hasn't happened to you?" I asked.

Richard thought that over.

A few weeks ago he came in again, or was brought in, for the same name calling and shoving. I sat down with him this time. I had not made an issue of it before. I talked to him about his "privileges." I told him it was no privilege at all and he knew it. He knew he had to come in early because he was not big enough to restrain himself outside. I added that, although he had told us often that he hated kindergarten, he should have learned some better ways of getting along with others, but since he hadn't, he would have to learn in the first grade. I don't remember what else I said, but Richard listened. We decided together that beginning the next day there would be no more privilege for him. He would come in with the others.

One morning, many weeks later, he came in with his class stopped at my desk and said,

"The service girls said I was to tell you I'm doing better in line."

I told him, "Good for you. I knew you could cooperate if you wanted to."

I cannot determine when our relationship changed significantly but there is a major difference since the early weeks of school. He used to challenge everything I had to say. This was all right. We differed. I had my ideas which I argued and he argued his. I sometimes told him, "Richard, you got up before I did this morning, now quiet down until I catch up with you." Sometimes he did, other times I was on my own. Occasionally I told him he had been most annoying and that if he could think of anything on his own to help the situation to go ahead and do it. At the time he was tolerantly accepting of me. But now we are friends and we both know it.

He is a stern critic of his own work. If it is not good and he asks me about it, I'll tell him I have seen him do much better. Sometimes he even does it over again, until he is satisfied.

One last incident. Of course, the children are excited about Christmas and Richard even more than the others, although he denies it. He was asked to step out of the room last week "Just until you can settle down and relax." While he was out in the hall he switched all the boots around. When he came back in, he told me what he had done. I said "good," playing the "game" with him. But at lunch time I discovered it was no game.

From many voices, I heard, "Mrs. King, I can't find my boots. I have two for the same foot and I can't find the other. Richard mixed them all up."

I called, "Richard, come here and straighten out these boots, please."

By this time everyone was complaining, even children whose boots he hadn't touched. It took Richard about three minutes and he had them all matched, but the accusations were still being voiced loudly. So I announced,

"If there's anything I like, it's a boy who can straighten out his own messes."

"And that's me," said Richard.

Mrs. Lawrence Confronts Her Group

Over a period of many months, a fairly successful teacher-indoctrination or "brainwashing" has been executed in this group on the joys of research study and the woeful disadvantages of using just one text book for their work. But, some place along the line another job of "thinking and speaking for yourself, expressing your own conviction" has been running a strong counter course! Like a regiment in ambush they spring one quiet day; almost united to a man on the pleasure they would derive from having a text, a single book, with discussion questions and problem exercises, "Like the other kids." Being kicked in the stomach might have been less painful to me at that moment; and to save the sinking ship and the drowning crew, I pulled out all the stops.

"Have you no appreciation of the value of looking at things more than one way? Can't you see the *fun* you could have putting ideas together from many phases of American life and from many different sources? What about the legends, literature, art, music, and dances of your people," I stormed. "Can't you draw some conclusions of your own? Must you have it crammed down your throats from the pages of one little book and one dictating teacher."—And for a final "pièce de resistance," in words to this effect; or more accurately, in these very words, I said, "You are all just plain lazy! You want to be spoon fed."

Well, there was hardly a dry eye in the house; the little scene I had staged had brought about the desired effect! Proud? Well, at that moment perhaps, but still rational enough to add; "You needn't decide now what to do; but tomorrow I will expect to have you indicate on a slip of paper if you prefer to have the textbook for the year, or if you would prefer to work together from many resources and research methods toward some meaningful insights and conclusions.

When my shaking stopped, and I sat in my empty classroom, I began thinking of the ugliness of the whole thing! This is teaching? Victory at any cost? It didn't take too long for me to realize that some of the very people who mattered most must now wonder if they really knew me as an honest self. Where was the consistency of my values now?

I can't honestly say that I knew what I was going to do about it when I walked into class the next day; in spite of the long night's struggle and post-mortem of the confrontation, but I applied, through no advanced plan of my own, the age old principle of apologizing when you know you have done something wrong. I held to my belief in the value of the resources, methods and principles we had used in the past months, but I admitted temporary irrationalism and professed that my lack of respect for their opinions was inexcusable! If it would afford them a better opportunity to state their views, and if it wasn't too late, I suggested a discussion. Everyone had something to say and the cleansing power of my words resulted in a completely different classroom atmosphere and a heightened sense of group solidarity. My pleasure in being a part of this was only commensurated with the knowledge that I had learned far more than any child in the room from this experience.

The Encounter

Every confrontation is an encounter but not every encounter is a confrontation. The encounter may not involve a dispute or controversy whereas the confrontation always contains some conflict. The encounter may be a sudden entering into the life of another in harmony and communion. It is a direct meeting between two persons who happen to come together. It may be an exchange of brief duration, a meeting with a total stranger. Yet in such a meeting there is full human intimacy and depth. Sometimes the brief encounter is a simple coming together of two faces or pairs of eyes, a sudden sense of knowing and being within the other, a feeling of harmony, unity, and continuity where all subject-object, self-other, individual-universal dichotomies disappear. The encounter is an immediate, imminent reality between two persons engaged in a living communion, where there is an absolute related-ness and sense of mutuality. As Buber (3, 203-204) says, " . . . if I and another come up against one another, 'happen' to one another, the sun does not exactly divide, there is a remainder, where the souls end and the world has not yet begun, and this is what is essen-tial. . . . In the most powerful moments of dialogue, where in truth 'deep calls unto deep,' it becomes unmistakably clear that it is not the word of the individual or the social, but of a third which draws the circle round the happening. On the far side of the subjective, on this side of the objective, on the narrow ridge, where *I* and *Thou* meet, there is a realm of 'between.' "

Whatever a man says or does, however alienated, detached and unrelated he may become, there remains within him forever an entirely unique and particular substance which is his own, which is intact and inviolate, and which can be recognized and called forth in an encounter with another person or with some form, object, or substance of the universe.

Every aspect of nature and life contains its own part of originality which comes into being, which is created and attains a living unity and persistence of form through encounters with other identities and forms.

Every encounter is significant, even though its meaning is hidden. In Hasidism and Modern Man, Buber expresses the value of the encounter in our daily living. He writes (4, p. 173), "The people we live with or meet with, the animals that help us with our farm work, the soil we till, the materials we shape, the tools we use, they all contain a mysterious spiritual substance which depends on us for helping it toward its pure form, its perfection. If we neglect this spiritual substance sent across our path, if we think only in terms of monetary purposes, without developing a genuine relationship to the beings and things in whose life we ought to take part, as they in ours, then we shall ourselves be debarred from true, fulfilled existence."

The encounter is a creative experience, in which there is a dropping off of all conventions, systems, rubrics, and a letting go so that one enters into the reality of a situation in terms of the conditions and requirements intrinsic to that situation. Openness, receptiveness, and relatedness are significant aspects of encounter with the world. There is a free and open play of attention, thought, feeling, perception. At a glance, frontiers of human experience become creative, revealing hitherto unknown vistas (11, p. 240). The openness and intensity of interest may range all the way from the grave and serious, the absorbing and tantalizing, to the playful and the fleeting (11, p. 242).

The encounter is not the fortuitous meeting or first coming together of two individuals, but rather the decisive inner experience which unfolds, in which something totally new is revealed, in which new horizons are opened (8, p. 119).

Intuitively, in the encounter, the person enters into a meaningful tie where mental power and compassion mingle. One cannot fruitfully meet the others unless he loves, impartially, selflessly, for love alone.

Haiku poems of Zen poets are expressions of an encounter between man and nature. Basho (1644-1694) was the first poet to crystallize the style. The following poems of Basho clearly reveal the experience of the encounter of man and the universe.

Black cloudbank broken
Scatters in the
Night . . . Now see
Moon-lighted Mountains! (2)

Now in Sad Autumn
Taking this my
Darkening path
Solitary bird. (2)
   ---Japanese Haiku. Peter Pauper
     Press, Mount Vernon, N.Y. 1955.

When I look carefully
I see the *nazuna* blooming
By the hedge! (1)

    This last poem is discussed by Suzuki in his lectures on Zen Buddhism. In analyzing the Haiku, Suzuki (12, p. 1-2) believes that Basho's love for nature stirred him when he discovered the inconspicuous, almost neglible plant blooming by the hedge. Basho happens upon the plant, looks at it, relates to it in all its fullness and tenderness. The very humbleness of the plant, its unpretentious beauty, evokes deep admiration. Basho sees the flower from the inside. Momentarily, he is the flower and lives its life. He has no words to utter; his feeling is too full, too deep and he has no desire to conceptualize it. His relation with the nazuna is one of harmony where color, tone, order, and grace combine to make a total creation.

    In all the above poems of Basho there is a depth of feeling, a mystery of utterance, an absolute subjectivity, meaningful only to those who have actually experienced what is revealed in these specific encounters with nature.

    Martin Buber (3, p. 112-113) relates an encounter between educator and student, which occurs when a young teacher faces his class for the first time. Vacillating between issuing orders immediately and setting up rules and standards, the teacher suddenly encounters a face in the crowd, a face which strikes him. It is not a beautiful face. But it is a real face and though it contains an expression of chaos, on the face the teacher reads a question: "Who are you? Do you know something that concerns me?"

I quote now the passage continuing this encounter:

In some such way he reads the question. And he, the young teacher, addresses this face. He says nothing very ponderous or important, he puts an ordinary introductory question: "What did you talk about last in geography? The Dead Sea? Well, what about the Dead Sea?" But there was obviously something not quite usual in the question, for the answer he gets is not the ordinary school boy answer; the boy begins to *tell a story*. Some months earlier he had stayed for a few hours on the shores of the Dead Sea and it is of this he tells. He adds: "And everything looked to me as if it had been created a day before the rest of creation." Quite unmistakably he had only in this moment made up his mind to talk about it. In the meantime his face has changed. It is no longer quite as chaotic as before. And the class has fallen silent. They all listen. The class, too, is no longer a chaos. Something has happened. The young teacher has started from above.

No matter how complicated or restricted or frightening a situation is, the opportunity for encounter is always present. However heavy the schedule, narrow the curriculum, or large the class size, whatever pressures or responsibilities the teacher faces, there is no way for another person to prevent the teacher from genuine meetings with a child. Only the teacher himself can decide. However momentary the encounters may be in the classroom, freedom to choose remains and can never be removed. The issue is not the person against the subject, but rather a choice of being or non-being. No matter how dictatorial or threatening the atmosphere of a school, the teacher can choose to be, can engender a spirit of human freedom while complying with rules and standards. If the teacher fails to choose to honor his own experience, fails to maintain a meaningful life as a teacher, the sense of estrangement and the anxiety of self-alienation will persist. Man is forever responsible for himself in his relations with others. And the guilt and shame one feels when one is not living authentically will continue to stun the person into a search for meaning and value in real encounters with life.

Claude and Mrs. Jensen

In a sustained relationship over the school year, Mrs. Jensen engaged in numerous encounters with Claude. She wrote these experiences as they occurred while they were still fresh and alive within her. I present this narrative below:

During his first day in second grade, Claude gave little indication of the deep well of anxiety which was to overflow during the days following. I felt with the boy the apprehensions normal to any child in a new school situation. He was surrounded by 30 unfamiliar children plus a teacher who was a total stranger. Our first day as a group was a pleasant experience spent sharing summer fun, general orientation to second grade work, and beginning the process of knowing each other.

Starting with the second day and continuing for months, however, Claude was often in tears. Accompanying the tears were fits of head pounding, desk thumping, feet kicking and book throwing. Each time I assigned work, it seemed I inflicted a new injury. For him it represented an insurmountable obstacle. He was snowed under by a feeling of desperate bewilderment and a defeated self-concept. His frustrated exhibitionism shocked other children. Fascinated, they watched, wide-eyed, listening without comment.

Countless times a day, at his first signs of anxiety, I faced him, speaking gently, "I know it's real hard for you, Claude, but try. I'll help you when you need help," or "This is giving you lots of trouble, but don't give up. I know you'll figure it out." He invariably responded with loud sobs and screams, "I won't get it. I can't! I can't!"

Day after day, for weeks I approached him with the same patience, waited for him to develop confidence in himself and improve in his skills. Gradually he at least attempted to do his work. But at each impasse, he turned to his own interests: drawing, looking at books, wandering about the room. While the head pounding and book throwing tapered off, he covered his desk with dark crayon scrawlings during moments of anxiety. I ignored this behavior, and, as if by magic, his desk would be cleaned off the next day.

When it was time for him to be with the group for guided reading, he was off by himself in a corner looking at supplementary readers or studying a science reference book. At first there were comments by other children, such as, "Claude is supposed to be in reading class now." To those comments, I replied, "Claude *is* in reading class. Let's let him read where he is. When he's ready, he'll join us, I'm sure." One day, of his own accord, he did come with the group. He has never failed since. My faith in waiting for him was rewarded.

Spelling tests, sentence dictation, reading workbooks, or any activity requiring his working with the group, continued to trigger a blast-off of emotions. I never graded his tests, workbooks, papers. Only the number correct were indicated. When he complained, I exclaimed, "You are worrying about what you do wrong. I suggest you look at all the things you do well."

I am deeply and forever grateful to my group of children who intuitively realized Claude needed their help and understanding. Without their spontaneous priceless gems, "I'll help you, Claude. Don't get so mad, Claude. Everyone makes mistakes," and "It is hard, but now if you'll just try . . ", I could not have lived through his explosions. Their genuine child-to-child relationships when helping him work with his tasks or playing with him, I know gave Claude strength and courage. The children understood without my ever informing them. They helped him to find in himself assurance and confidence in his ability to achieve.

His creativeness and giftedness in art were soon spotted by others. Their words, "Gee, Claude, you're the best drawer in the room" was the boost he needed.

In the beginning, Claude's anxieties were not confined to the classroom alone. They were expressed in different ways—on the playground, the lunch line, school environs. His aggressiveness, roughness, and lack of consideration of others, brought complaints not only from his classmates but from others as well. In a short time he made a cruel discovery: the realization that he had no friends. "No one wants to play with me. They don't like me," he cried. So we discussed fair play, bossing, sharing, consideration of others, taking turns, being good sports. We looked at the conflict which occurred. He did most of the talking and little by little, through his own efforts, the accepted and reasonable ways of playing with other children became a part of him, too.

One November incident on the playground almost crushed our relationship. The playground was wet with slush. I watched Claude as he went skidding along, with Larry after him. Suddenly Claude fell, getting one of his trouser legs wet. As I walked toward him, he ran to me, screaming over and over, "Larry pushed me! I'm all wet! My Ma'll whip me!" Larry stood by saying, "But, Claude, I didn't push you."

I asked Claude to go indoors. As we came back to the classroom we were greeted by Claude running up to Larry, screaming, "You're a liar! A liar! A liar! You pushed me!" "But Claude," I started to say, . . . He turned on me in rage, shouting, "You're a liar, too! A GREAT BIG LIAR! He did push me! He did! He did! He did!" I had a momentary impulse to shake him. But had I done so, all would have been undone . . . the faith, the trust, his security with me. When I looked, I saw him and his human plight for the first time. It registered deep down inside me, his hysterical screams, his pitiful tears, his wild, accusing eyes, and the rest of his classmates staring condemningly at him. "All right, Claude," I said quietly. "It's all right. Scream and shout if you must. I'm here. I'll listen. When you're through I want you to take your seat." Without saying another word, he slumped in his chair.

He put his head down. We went on with our work. I noticed when Claude finally raised his head that his desk was wet. I could see his agony. At the same time our eyes met, and he looked at me lovingly through silent tears.

As usual at dismissal time, I stood at the door of our classroom as the children left. Claude started to pass, his face white and smudged with dried tears. He hesitated momentarily. Our eyes met again. I cupped his face in my hand. I said, "We've had a rough afternoon, but it's all over now. There's a *good* day coming Monday. Have fun 'til I see you then." His head went down, he leaned against me, and he said in a small voice, "I won't scream at you ever again."

By Christmas time his frequency of upsets had become fewer and fewer. With help over the rough spots his academic work had improved steadily. He was chosen by the class to be the chairman of the group responsible for decorating the large bulletin board across the back of the room. He chose the nativity scene, organized his helpers, selected all the colored paper to be used, made a sketch of the scene, and decided what each person was to draw. He was happy and glowing as he worked many hours after his regular assignments had been completed. He helped others with ideas and did a great deal of the drawing himself. The scene was truly beautiful and complete in every detail. But even more beautiful was the relationship that grew between Claude and me during the nights he stayed after school working on the nativity scene.

It was during those moments that he poured forth his feelings ... how he always thought he couldn't do anything "good" ... how he felt at the other school ... how because he was the oldest of six children at home and had to do everything, he was whipped for not doing things right ... how his brother always bothered him, forcing him to hide away with his dog ... how at the other school he fell, hitting his head on a stone, and had to go to the hospital many times for checkups. He bared his very being to me. Surely, I thought, this is the wonder and ecstacy of relatedness when hostility and hatred become concern and love.

Don't be misled into believing that there have been no anxious moments. But they are so infrequent and mild compared to those of last September that they are quickly and easily dissolved by Claude himself with little help from me. He is now a happy boy, well liked by his many friends, a good student and school citizen. Every time I see him, I am thrilled that I could relate to him as a genuine person.

Before closing, I will present an illustration of an encounter which modified in a significant way my relations with adults, particularly my capacity to bear pain and suffering, and my awareness and sensitivity to loneliness as a value in life. The experience involves an old man who hates himself and wants to die and a young man who quickly feels his pain and wants to live, to be with him in the most crushing illness of his life.

Communal Loneliness

He stood in the doorway of my office, a terribly stooped old man. Pain and misery, heavy wrinkles, lined his face. He stared beyond me, fiery, piercing eyes fixed to the floor, a face filled with indescribable loneliness and defeat. 'Won't you come in and sit down,' I asked gently. He entered the room, but he did not sit. He began to pace, back and forth. Increasingly, I felt the turbulence inside him which electrified my office with a kind of frozen tension. The tension mounted, becoming almost unbearable. Heavy beads of perspiration fell from his face and forehead. Tears filled his eyes. He started to speak several times but the words would not come. He stroked his hair roughly and pulled at his clothing. The pacing continued.

I felt his suffering keenly, deep inside me, spreading throughout my whole body. I remarked, "So utterly painful and lonely." "Lonely," he cried, "Lonely! Lonely!" he shouted, "I've been alone all my life." He spoke in rasping tones, his nerves drawn taut. "I've never been an honest person. I've never done anything I really wanted to, nothing I truly believed in. I don't know what I believe in anymore. I don't know what I feel. I don't know what to do with myself. I wish I could die . . . how I have yearned, how I have longed for death to come, to end this misery. If I had the courage, I would kill myself. These headaches. Have you ever known such lasting pain? I don't know how much more I can stand. I haven't slept for months. I wake up in the middle of the night. Everything is dark, black, ugly, empty. Right now my head is throbbing. I take pills. I try to rest. I avoid becoming upset. Nothing helps. My head is splitting. I don't think I can take this pain much longer. I wake with a start. My heart fills with terror. My wife and children are asleep, with me in the house—but I am entirely alone. I am not a father. I am not a husband. I'm no one. Look! See these tears" I could weep forever. Forever. I sometimes feel I cry for the whole world—a world that's sour and lost."

All this the old man uttered—sobbing, choking, sighing, gasping for breath. The sounds were thick. His tongue was fastened to his gums. Only with the greatest effort did he talk. It was almost unendurable. The lacinating physical pain and mental anguish mounted unrelentlessly. There was not even a moment of suspension so we could breathe normally and recapture our resources. His distress was cumulative, increasingly exhaustive.

In his completely weakened state, unknown urges, unknown capacities, a surprising strength enabled him to continue. From the beginning he had never been a real person. It was too late now, he felt. Nothing in life was real. For seventy-four years he had lived by other people's descriptions of him, others' perceptions of him. He had come to believe that this was his real self. He had become timid and shy, when he might have discovered and developed social interests. He was silent when he might have something to say. He played cards every Tuesday and attended club meetings every Thursday when he might have enjoyed being alone, or conversing with his wife, or developing an avocation or hobby. He listened to the radio and watched television every evening when he might have discovered values in music and books. He did not know his real interests and talents, his real aspirations and goals. He never gave himself time to discover himself.

He asked in agony, "Do you know what it means not to feel anything, to be completely alone and without feeling? Do you understand what it is to know only pain and loneliness? My family doesn't understand me. They think I have these headaches because my business is failing. They think I roam the house at night, moving from bed to couch to chair to floor, because I'm worrying about my business. They think I am worrying about new possibilities and plans. So they soften me and treat me gingerly. Husband and father must have a quiet house, so the house is quiet. He must not be upset, so he is avoided. He must not be expected to be friendly and sociable because he is passive and shy. He must be indirectly talked into doing what they want, in the right way, at the right moment. It takes careful planning. He must have sympathy, even if it's false, to be able to face the tough, competitive world outside. They cannot and will not recognize that this man they handle with kid gloves, whom they fear upsetting, whom they decide has to be coddled and manipulated into buying new clothes, a new car, a new home, all the other possessions a family feels it must have, this man does not really exist and never did. But who is he? He doesn't know and he doesn't know how to find out. Can't you see? I do not really exist. I am nothing. Do you know what it is not to know how you feel, not to know your own thoughts, not to know what you believe, not to know what you want, not to be sure of anything but endless pain and suffering? And everyone else takes you for granted, on already formed opinions and actions, the same words, the same ways. How do I start to live again? I'm dying and I can't stop breathing. I can't stop living."

These were the themes of our talks together—self-denial, estrangement, rejection, excruciating pain, spreading loneliness. We met eight times. In each visit, his suffering and sense of isolation increased, reaching unbelievable heights. Often, I thought, "Surely this is it. He has reached the breaking point." He seemed at the very end of his power and resources. But he kept coming until I wondered whether I had not reached the breaking point. The only thing that kept me going was the certainty that without me there would be no one—no one at all. I could not give up, abandon him, even when I questioned my own strength to continue to live through our conversations and the lonely terror not expressible in words. I suffered deeply in these hours with him. Each time he came I felt on the verge of sinking into total despair. Often when he wept, there were tears in my eyes too, and when his head ached painfully, I felt the pain all the way through me. And when he paced and pulled at himself, I felt a terrible restlessness and agitation. And when he was utterly alone and lonely, I was alone and lonely, too. My full, complete presence was not enough to alleviate his suffering, his self-lacerating expressions. I felt an awful loneliness and desolation as I was not able to help him find a beginning, locate a direction a new pathway of relatedness to himself and others. It hurt me deeply to see him grow increasingly, unbelievably tortured and not be able to help him find a meaning or even some beginning belief in the possibility of a good life. He was dying before me and something within me was dying too. I could not reach him. I do not know what effort of will power, what inner strivings of the heart, what forces kept me going in the face of this unendurable, mounting desolation, despair, and loneliness. I felt defeated and weakened, yet each time he came I met him squarely, honestly, directly. Each time my capacity for bearing with him seemed to be reaching a terminal point, new threads inside revived me. Somehow fresh strength flowed into me, mysteriously encouraging me and enabling me to continue. I listened to him and believed in him. I was convinced he had the power within himself to find a new meaning to life. I continued to live with him in the crucial hours of psychic dying. My entire office filled with his aching. I could feel it everywhere in the room—in the floor, the walls, the furniture, the papers and books on my desk. It settled irrevocably and held stationary. For some time after he left, I did not move. I remained heavy as the feeling he left when he departed.

Then on the ninth appointment he did not come. What could this defection mean? How had I failed? Had he sensed my own growing struggle, my own exhaustion, my own loneliness? I searched within myself and within our relations but I could find no satisfactory answer.

Two weeks passed before he called. He spoke in a calm voice, in a totally different way from any previous words. "It's all so fresh and raw," he said, "and so new and startling that I'm constantly uncertain, but I feel I am coming into a totally new existence. I sometimes doubt that what I am feeling will last, but the feelings persisted now almost two weeks and I'm beginning to recognize them as my own. I do not know what is happening or how, but by some strange miracle or inner working, I am beginning to breathe again and to live again. I do not want to see you just now because I must have further confirmation, but I will call you soon."

Six weeks later the old man came for the last time. I could barely recognize him. He looked youthful. His face was alive. His smile was radiant and so thrilling I felt tingling sensations everywhere inside me. He spoke warmly, confidently, "I came only to see your face light up, to be warmed by the gleam in your eyes. I know how much you suffered. I have seen your tortured face even after leaving you. I'll just sit here with you quietly a few minutes." So we sat in silence, each revelling in the birth, each warmed by a bond that emerged from deep and spreading roots in the hours of anguish and loneliness. We were no longer alone or lonely. We had found a new strength and sustenance in each other.

The fundamental communion in which we suffered enabled him to get to the very depths of his experience. Perhaps in arriving at the foundation of his grief and loneliness, immediate death or immediate life were the only choices within reach. He chose to live. From his rock bottom loneliness emerged a new life and a real self was restored.

Martin Buber has caught my feeling from this experience, exactly, in the following passage from Hasidism and Modern Man (4, p. 120-121) as follows:

" . . . not to help out of pity, that is, out of a sharp, quick pain which one wishes to expel, but out of love, that is, out of living with the other. He who pities does not live with the suffering of the sufferer, he does not bear it in his heart as one bears the life of a tree with all its drinking in and shooting forth and with the dream of its roots and the craving of its trunk and the thousand journeys of its branches, or as one bears the life of an animal with all its gliding, stretching, and grasping and all the joy of its sinews and its joints and the dull tension of its brain. He does not bear in his heart this special essence, the suffering of the other; rather he receives from the most external features of this suffering a sharp, quick pain, unbridgeably dissimilar to the original pain of the sufferer. And it is thus that he is moved. But the helper must live with the other, and only help that arises out of living with the other can stand before the eyes of God."

References

1. Arishima, Takeo, *A Cluster of Grapes.* Translated by Kazuko Yoshinaga. Detroit: Merrill—Palmer Institute, 1960.
2. Basho, *Japanese Haiku.* Mount Vernon, New York: Peter Pauper Press, 1955.
3. Buber, Martin. *Between Man and Man.* London: Routledge and Kegan Paul Ltd., 1947.
4. Buber, Martin. *Hasidism and Modern Man.* New York: Horizon Press, 1958.
5. Buber, Martin. *I and Thou.* Edinburgh, Scotland: T. & T. Clark, 1937.
6. Cousins, Norman. "The Desensitization of Twentieth-Century Man." *The Saturday Review*, May 16, 1959.
7. Frankl, Viktor E. *From Death-Camp to Existentialism.* Boston: Beacon Press, 1959.
8. May, Rollo; Angel, Ernest; Ellenberger, Henri F., (Editors). *Existence: A New Dimension in Psychiatry and Psychology.* New York: Basic Books, 1958.
9. Moustakas, Clark E. *Loneliness.* Unpublished Manuscript. Detroit: Merrill-Palmer Institute, 1960.
10. Moustakas, Clark E. *Psychotherapy with Children: The Living Relationship.* New York: Harper and Brothers, 1959.
11. Schachtel, Ernest G. *Metamorphosis.* New York: Basic Books, 1959.
12. Suzuki, D.T., Fromm, Erich; DeMartino, Richard. *Zen Buddhism and Psychoanalysis.* New York: Harper and Brothers, 1960.

10. Why Teachers Fail

B.F. Skinner

The most widely publicized efforts to improve education show an extraordinary neglect of method. Learning
and teaching are not analyzed, and almost no effort is
made to improve teaching as such. The aid which education is to receive usually means money, and the proposals for spending it follow a few, familiar lines. We
should build more and better schools. We should recruit
more and better teachers. We should search for better
students and make sure that all competent students can
go to school or college. We should multiply teacher-
student contacts with films and television. We should
design new curricula. All this can be done without looking at teaching itself. We need not ask how those better
teachers are to teach those better students in those better schools, what kinds of contact are to be multiplied
through mass media, or how new curricula are to be
made effective.

Perhaps we should not expect questions of this sort
to be asked in what is essentially a consumer's revolt.
Earlier educational reforms were proposed by
teachers—a Comenius, a Rousseau, a John Dewey—who
were familiar with teaching methods, knew their shortcomings, and thought they saw a chance to improve
them. Today the disaffected are the parents, employers,
and others who are unhappy about the products of education. When teachers complain, it is as consumers of

Saturday Review, 40 (No. 42): 80-81, 98 ff., October 16, 1965. Copyright © 1965 Saturday Review, Inc. Reprinted by permission of the author
and the *Saturday Review*.

education at lower levels—graduate school authorities want better college teaching, college teachers work to improve high-school curricula, and so on. It is perhaps natural that consumers should turn to the conspicuous shortcomings of plant, personnel, and equipment rather than to method.

It is also true that educational method has not been brought to their attention in a favorable light. Pedagogy is not a prestigious word. Its low estate may be traced in part to the fact that under the blandishments of statistical methods, which promised a new kind of rigor, educational psychologists spent half a century measuring the results of teaching while neglecting teaching itself. They compared different methods of teaching in matched groups and could often say that one method was clearly better than another, but the methods they compared were usually not drawn from their own research or even their own theories, and their results seldom generated new methods. Psychological studies of learning were equally sterile—concentrating on relatively unimportant details of a few typical learning situations such as the memory drum, the maze, the discrimination box, and verbal "problems." The learning and forgetting curves that emerged from these studies were never useful in the classroom and came to occupy a less and less important place in textbooks on educational psychology. Even today many distinguished learning theorists insist that their work has no practical relevance.

For these and doubtless other reasons, what has been taught as pedagogy has not been a true technology of teaching. College teaching, indeed, has not been taught at all. The beginning teacher receives no professional preparation. He usually begins to teach simply as he himself has been taught, and if he improves, it is only in the light of his own unaided experience. High-school and grade-school teaching is taught primarily through apprenticeships, in which students receive the advice and counsel of experienced teachers. Certain trade skills and rules of thumb are passed along, but the young teacher's own experience is to be the major source of improvement. Even this modest venture in teacher training is under attack. It is argued that a good teacher is simply one who knows his subject matter and is interested in it. Any special knowledge of pedagogy as a basic science of teaching is felt to be unnecessary.

The attitude is regrettable. No enterprise can improve itself to the fullest extent without examining its basic processes. A really effective educational system cannot be set up until we understand the processes of learning and teaching. Human behavior is far too complex to be left to casual experience, or even to organized experience in the restricted environment of the classroom. Teachers need help. In particular they need the kind of help offered by a scientific analysis of behavior.

Fortunately such an analysis is now available. Principles derived from it have already contributed to the design of schools, equipment, texts, and classroom practices. Programmed instruction is, perhaps, its best known achievement. Some acquaintance with its basic formulation is beginning to be regarded as important in the training of teachers and administrators. These positive contributions, however, are no more important than the light which the analysis throws on current practices. There is something wrong with teaching. From the point of view of an experimental analysis of behavior, what is it?

Corporal punishment, which has always played an important role in education, provides one clue. As H.I. Marrou says in *A History of Education in Antiquity:* "Education and corporal punishment appeared as inseparable to a Hellenistic Greek as they had to a Jewish or an Egyptian scribe in the time of the Pharoahs . . . When the men of antiquity thought back to their schooldays they immediately remembered the beatings." The cane is still with us, and efforts to abolish it are vigorously opposed. In Great Britain a split leather strap for whipping students called a taws can be obtained from suppliers who advertise in educational journals, one of whom is said to sell 3,000 annually. (The taws has the advantage, shared by the rubber truncheon, of leaving no incriminating marks.)

The brutality of corporal punishment and the viciousness it breeds in both teacher and student have, of course, led to reform. Usually this has meant little more

than shifting to noncorporal measures, of which education can boast an astonishing list. Ridicule (now largely
verbalized, but once symbolized by the dunce cap or by
forcing the student to sit facing a wall), scolding, sarcasm, criticism, incarceration (being "kept after
school"), extra school or home work, the withdrawal of
privileges, forced labor, ostracism, being put on silence,
and fines—these are some of the devices that have permitted the teacher to spare the rod without spoiling the
child. In some respects they are less objectionable than
corporal punishment, but the pattern remains: the student spends a great part of his day doing things he does
not want to do. If a teacher is in any doubt about his
own methods, he should ask himself a few questions. Do
my students stop work immediately when I dismiss the
class? (If so, dismissal is obviously a release from a
threat.) Do they welcome rather than regret vacations
and unscheduled days of no school? Do I reward them
for good behavior by excusing them from other assignments? Do I punish them by giving them additional
assignments? Do I frequently say, "Pay attention,"
"Now remember," or otherwise gently "admonish"
them? Do I find it necessary from time to time to "get
tough" and threaten some form of punishment?

The teacher can use aversive control because he is
either bigger and stronger than his students or able to
invoke the authority of parents or police who are. He
can coerce students into reading texts, listening to lectures, taking part in discussions, recalling as much as
possible of what they have read or heard, writing papers,
and so on. This is perhaps an achievement, but it is
offset by an extraordinary list of unwanted by-products
traceable to the basic practice.

The student who works mainly to escape aversive
stimulation discovers other ways of escaping. He is
tardy—"creeping like snail unwilling to school." He
stays away from school altogether. Education has its
own word for this—"truancy"—from an old Celt word
meaning wretched. A special policeman, the truant officer, deals with offenders by threatening still more aversive consequences. The dropout is a legal truant. Children who commit suicide are often found to have had
trouble in school.

There are subtler forms of escape. Though physically present and looking at teacher or text, the student does not pay attention. He is hysterically deaf. His mind wanders. He daydreams. "Mental fatigue" is usually not a state of exhaustion but an uncontrollable disposition to escape, and schools deal with it by permitting escape to other activities that, it is hoped, will also be profitable. The periods into which the school day is broken measure the limits of successful aversive control rather than the capacity for sustained attention. A child who will spend hours absorbed in play or in watching movies or television cannot sit still in school for more than a few minutes before escape becomes too strong to be denied. One of the easiest forms of escape is simply to forget all one has learned, and no one has discovered a form of control to prevent this ultimate break for freedom.

An equally serious result which an experimental analysis of behavior leads us to expect is that students counter-attack. If the teacher is weak, the student may attack openly. Physical attacks on teachers are now common. Verbal attacks in the teacher's absence are legendary. When the teacher is present, attacks may take the form of annoyance, and students escape punishment by annoying surreptitiously—by groaning, shuffling the feet, or snapping the fingers. A "tormenter" was a surreptitious noise maker especially designed for classroom use.

Counter-attack escalates. Slightly aversive action by the teacher evokes reactions that demand severer measures, to which in turn the student reacts still more violently. Escalation may continue until one party withdraws (the student leaves school or the teacher resigns) or dominates completely (the students establish anarchy or the teacher imposes a despotic discipline.)

Vandalism is another form of counter-attack that is growing steadily more serious. Many cities maintain special police forces to guard school buildings on weekends. Schools are now being designed so that windows cannot be easily broken from the street. A more sweeping counter-attack comes later when, as taxpayers or alumni, former students refuse to support educational institutions. Anti-intellectualism is often a general attack on all that education represents.

A much less obvious but equally serious effect of aversive control is plain inaction. The student is sullen and unresponsive. He "blocks." Inaction is sometimes a form of escape. Rather than carry out an assignment, the student simply takes punishment as the lesser evil. It is sometimes a form of attack, the object of which is to enrage the teacher. But it is also in its own right a predictable effect of aversive control.

All these reactions have emotional accompaniments. Fear and anxiety are characteristic of escape and avoidance, anger of counter-attack, and resentment of sullen inaction. These are the classical features of juvenile delinquency, of psychosomatic illness, and of other maladjustments familiar to the administrations and health services of educational institutions.

In college and graduate schools the aversive pattern survives in the now almost universal system of "assign and test." The teacher does not teach, he simply holds the student responsible for learning. The student must read books, study texts, perform experiments, and attend lectures, and he is responsible for doing so in the sense that, if he does not correctly report what he has seen, heard, or read, he will suffer aversive consequences. Questions and answers are so staple a feature of education that their connection with teaching almost never occasions surprise, yet as a demand for a response that will meet certain specifications, a question is almost always slightly aversive. An examination, as a collection of questions, characteristically generates the anxiety and panic appropriate to avoidance and escape. Reading a student's paper is still likely to be called "correcting" it. Examinations are designed to show principally what the student does *not* know. A test that proves to be too easy is made harder before being given again, ostensibly because an easy test does not discriminate, but more probably because the teacher is afraid of weakening the threat under which his students are working. A teacher is judged by his employers and colleagues by the severity of the threat he imposes: he is a good teacher if he makes his students work hard, regardless of how he does so or of how much he teaches them by doing so. He eventually evaluates himself in the same way; if he tries to shift to nonaversive methods, he may discover that he resists making things easy as if this necessarily meant teaching less.

Proposals to add requirements and raise standards are usually part of an aversive pattern. A well known educator has written: "We must stiffen the work of our schools . . . we have every reason to concentrate on [certain subjects] and be unflagging in our insistence that they be really learned . . . Senior year [in high school] ought to be the hardest . . . [We should give] students work that is both difficult and important, and [insist] that it be well done . . . We should demand more of our students." These expressions were probably intended to be synonymous with "students should learn more" or possibly "teachers should teach more." There may be good reasons why students should take more mathematics or learn a modern language more thoroughly or be better prepared for college or graduate school, but they are not reasons for intensifying aversive pressures. A standard is a level of achievement; only under a particular philosophy of education is it a criterion upon which some form of punishment is contingent.

Most teachers are humane and well disposed. They do not want to threaten their students, yet they find themselves doing so. They want to help, but their offers to help are often declined. Most students are well disposed. They want an education, yet they cannot force themselves to study, and they know they are wasting time. For reasons which they have probably not correctly identified, many are in revolt. Why should education continue to use the aversive techniques to which all this is so obviously due? Evidently because effective alternatives have not been found. It is not enough simply to abandon aversive measures. A Summerhill is therapeutic not educational. By withholding punishment teachers may help students who have been badly treated elsewhere and prepare them to be taught, but something else is needed if they are to teach. What is that something else, and why has it not yet solved the problem?

A child sees things and talks about them accurately afterward. He listens to news and gossip and passes it along. He recounts in great detail the plot of a movie he has seen or a book he has read. He seems to have a "natural curiosity," a "love of knowledge," and "inherent wish to learn." Why not take advantage of these natural endowments and simply bring the student into contact with the world he is to learn about? There are practical problems, of course. Only a small part of the real world can be brought into the classroom even with the aid of films, tape recorders, and television, and only a small part of what remains can be visited outside. Words are easily imported, but the verbal excesses of classical education have shown how easily this fact may lead to a dangerous overemphasis. Within reasonable limits, however, is it not possible to teach simply by giving the student an opportunity to learn in a natural way?

Unfortunately, a student does not learn simply when he is shown or told. Something essential to his natural curiosity to wish to learn is missing from the classroom. What is missing, technically speaking, is "positive reinforcement." In daily life the student looks, listens, and remembers because certain consequences then follow. He learns to look and listen in those special ways that encourage remembering because he is reinforced for recalling what he has seen and heard, just as a newspaper reporter notes and remembers things he sees because he is paid for reporting them. Consequences of this sort are lacking when a teacher simply shows a student something or tells him something.

Rousseau was the great advocate of natural learning. Emile was to be taught by the world of things. His teacher was to draw his attention to that world; but otherwise his education was to be negative. There were to be no arranged consequences. But Emile was an imaginary student with imaginary learning processes. When Rousseau's disciple, Pestalozzi, tried the methods of his own flesh-and-blood son, he ran into trouble. His diary is one of the most pathetic documents in the history of education. As he walked with his young son beside a stream, Pestalozzi would repeat several times, "Water flows downhill." He would show the boy that "wood swims in water and . . . stones sink." Whether the child was learning anything or not, he was not unhappy, and

Pestalozzi could believe that at least he was using the right method. But when the world of things had to be left behind, failure could no longer be concealed. "I could only get him to read with difficulty; he has a thousand ways of getting out of it, and never loses an opportunity of doing something else." He could make the boy sit still at his lessons by first making him "run and play out of doors in the cold," but Pestalozzi himself was then exhausted. Inevitably, of course, he returned to aversive measures: "He was soon tired of learning to read, but as I had decided that he should work at it regularly every day, whether he liked it or not, I determined to make him feel the necessity of doing so, from the very first, by showing him there was no choice between this work and my displeasure, which I made him feel by keeping him in."

The failure of "showing and telling" is sometimes attributed to lack of attention. We are often aware that we ourselves are not listening or looking carefully. If we are not to punish the student for not looking and not listening, how can we make him concentrate? One possibility is to make sure that there is nothing else to be seen or heard. The schoolroom is isolated and freed of distractions. Silence is often the rule. Physical constraints are helpful. Earphones reassure the teacher that only what is to be heard is going into the student's ear. The TV screen is praised for its isolation and hypnotic effect. A piece of equipment has been proposed that achieves concentration in the following desperate way: the student faces a brightly lighted text, framed by walls which operate on the principle of the blinders once worn by carriage horses. His ears are between earphones. He reads part of the text aloud and then listens to his recorded voice as he reads it again. If he does not learn what he reads, it is certainly not because he has not seen it!

A less coercive practice is to make what is to be seen or heard attractive and attention-compelling. The advertiser faces the same problem as the teacher, and his techniques have been widely copied in the design of textbooks, films, and classroom practices. Bright colors, variety, sudden change, big type, animated sequences—

all these have at least a temporary effect in inducing the student to look and listen. They do not, however, *teach* the student to look and listen, because they occur at the wrong time. A similar weakness is seen in making school itself pleasant. Attractive architecture, colorful interiors, comfortable furniture, congenial social arrangements, naturally interesting subjects—these are all reinforcing, but they reinforce only the behaviors they are contingent upon. An attractive school building reinforces the behavior of coming in sight of it. A colorful and comfortable classroom reinforces the behavior of entering it. Roughly speaking, these things could be said to strengthen a positive attitude toward school. But they provide merely the setting for instruction. They do not teach what students are in school to learn.

In the same way audiovisual aids usually come at the wrong time to strengthen the forms of behavior that are the principal concern of the teacher. An interesting page printed in four colors reinforces the student simply for opening the book and looking at it. It does not reinforce reading the page or even examining it closely; certainly it does not reinforce those activities that result in effective recall of what is seen. An interesting lecturer holds his listeners in the sense that they look at and listen to him, just as an interesting demonstration film reinforces the behavior of watching it, but neither the lecture nor the film necessarily reinforces listening or listening in those special ways that further recall. In good instruction interesting things should happen *after* the student has read a page or listened or looked with care. The four-color picture should *become* interesting when the text that accompanies it has been read. One stage in a lecture or film should be interesting only if earlier stages have been carefully examined and remembered. In general, naturally attractive and interesting things further the primary goals of education only when they enter into much more subtle contingencies of reinforcement than are usually represented by audiovisual aids.

It is possible that students may be induced to learn by making material not only attractive but memorable. An obvious example is making material easy. The child first learns to write in manuscript because it resembles

the text he is learning to read; he may learn to read
material printed in a phonetic alphabet; he may learn to
spell only words he will actually use; and so on. This
sort of simplification shows a lack of confidence in
methods of teaching and often merely postpones the
teacher's task, but it is sometimes a useful strategy.
Material which is well organized is also, of course, easier
to learn.

Some current psychological theories suggest that material may be made memorable in another way. Various
laws of perception imply that an observer "cannot help"
seeing things in certain ways. The stimulus seems to
force itself upon the organism. Optical illusions are
often cited as examples. These laws suggest the possibility that material may be presented in the form in which
it is irresistibly learned. Material is to be so "structured"
that it is readily—and almost necessarily—"grasped." Instructional examples are, however, far less persuasive
than the demonstration offered in support of them. In
trying to assign an important function to the material to
be learned, it is particularly easy to overlook other conditions under which learning actually occurs.

No matter how attractive, interesting, and well structured material may be, the discouraging fact is that it is
often not learned. Rather than continue to ask why,
many educational theorists have concluded that the
teacher cannot really teach at all but can only help the
student learn. The dominant metaphor goes back to
Plato. As Emile Brehier states it in *The Hellenic Age,*
"Socrates . . . possessed no other art but maieutics, his
mother Phaenarete's art of delivering; he drew out from
souls what they have in them . . ." The student already
knows the truth; the teacher simply shows him that he
knows. The archetype is the famous episode in the
Meno in which Socrates takes an uneducated slave boy
through Pythagoras's theorem for doubling the square.
In spite of the fact that this scene is still widely regarded
as an educational triumph, there is no evidence that the
child learned anything. He timidly agrees with various
suggestions, and he answers leading questions, but it is
inconceivable that he could have reconstructed the theorem by himself when Socrates had finished. Socrates

says as much later in the dialogue: "If someone will keep asking him these same questions often and in various forms, you can be sure that in the end he will know about them as accurately as anybody." (Socrates was a frequency theorist!)

It must be admitted that the assignment was difficult. The boy was starting from scratch. In this little book, *How to Solve It,* Polya uses the same technique in presiding at the birth of the formula for the diagonal of a parallelepiped. His students make a more positive contribution because they have already had some geometry. But any success due to previous teaching weakens the claim for maieutics. And Polya's promptings and questionings give more help than he wants to admit.

It is only because mathematical proofs seem to arise from the nature of things that they can be said in some sense to be "known by everyone" and simply waiting to be drawn out. Even Socrates could not argue that the soul knows the facts of history or a second language. Impregnation must precede parturition. But is it not possible that a presentation that has not seemed to be learned is the seed from which knowledge grows to be delivered by the teacher? Perhaps the intellectual midwife is to show the student that he remembers what he has already been shown or told. In *The Idea of a University* Cardinal Newman gave an example of the maieutic method applied to acquired knowledge. It will stir painful memories in many teachers. A tutor is talking with a candidate about a bit of history—a bit of history, in fact, in which Plato's Menon lost his life.

> "What is the meaning of the word *Anabasis*?" says the Tutor. The Candidate is silent. "You know very well; take your time, and don't be alarmed, *Anabasis* means . . ."
> "An ascent," says the Candidate.
> "*Who* ascended?"
> "The Greeks, Xenophon."
> "Very well: Xenophon and the Greeks ascended. To what did they ascend?"
> "Against the Persian king: they ascended to fight the Persian king."
> "That is right . . . an ascent; but I thought we called it a *de*scent when a foreign army carried war into a country? . . . "Don't we talk of a descent of barbarians?"
> "Yes."

"Why then are the Greeks said to go up?"

"They went up to fight the Persian king."

"Yes; but why *up* . . . why not *down*?"

"They came down afterwards, when they retreated back to Greece."

"Perfectly right; they did . . . but could you give no reason why they are said to go *up* to Persia, not *down*?"

"They went *up* to Persia."

"Why do you not say they went *down*?"

"They went *down* to Persia."

"You have misunderstood me . . . ."

Newman warned his reader that the Candidate is "deficient to a great extent . . . not such as it is likely that a respectable school would turn out." He recognized a poor student, but not a poor method. Thousands of teachers have wasted years of their lives in exchanges which have been no more profitable—and all to the greater glory of maieutics and out of a conviction that telling and showing are not only inadequate but wrong.

Although the soul has perhaps not always known the truth nor ever been confronted with it in a half-forgotten experience, it may still *seek* it. If the student can be taught to learn from the world of things, nothing else will ever have to be taught. This is the method of discovery. It is designed to absolve the teacher from a sense of failure by making instruction unnecessary. The teacher arranges the environment in which discovery is to take place, he suggests lines of inquiry, he keeps the student within bounds, and so on. The important thing is that he should tell him nothing.

The human organism does, of course, learn without being taught. It is a good thing that this is so, and it would no doubt be a good thing if more could be learned in that way. Students are naturally interested in what they learn by themselves because they would not learn if they were not, and for the same reason they are more likely to remember what they learn in that way. There are reinforcing elements of surprise and accomplishment in personal discovery that are welcome alternatives to traditional aversive consequences. But discovery is no solution to the problems of education. The individual cannot be expected to rediscover more than a very small part of the facts and principles that have already been discovered by others. To stop teaching in order that the student may learn for himself is to abandon education as a medium for the transmission of the accumulated knowledge and wisdom of a culture.

There are other difficulties. The position of the teacher who encourages discovery is ambiguous. Is he to pretend that he himself does not know? (Socrates said Yes. In Socratic irony those who know enjoy a laugh at the expense of those who do not.) Or, for the sake of encouraging a joint venture in discovery, is the teacher to choose to teach only those things that he himself has not yet learned? Or is he frankly to say, "I know, but you must find out" and accept the consequences for his relations with his students?

Still another difficulty arises when it is necessary to teach a whole class. How are a few good students to be prevented from making all the discoveries? When that happens, other members of the class not only miss the excitement of discovery but are left to learn material presented in a slow and particularly confusing way. Students should, of course, be encouraged to explore, to ask questions, to study by themselves, to be "creative." When properly analyzed, the kinds of behavior referred to in such expressions can be taught. It does not follow, however, that they must be taught by the method of discovery.

Effective, instructional practices threaten the conception of teaching as a form of maieutics. If we suppose that the student is to "exercise his rational powers," to "develop his mind," to learn through "intuition or insight," and so on, then it may indeed be true that the teacher cannot teach but can only help the student learn. But these goals can be restated in terms of explicit changes in behavior, and effective methods of instruction can then be designed.

In his famous four idols, Francis Bacon formulated some of the reasons why men arrive at false ideas. He might have added two special Idols of the School that affect those who want to improve teaching. The Idol of the Good Teacher is the belief that what a good teacher can do, any teacher can do. Some teachers are, of course, unusually effective. They are naturally interesting people, who make things interesting to their students. They are skillful in handling students, as they are skillful in handling people in general. They can formulate facts and principles and communicate them to others in effective ways. Possibly their skills and talents will someday be better understood and successfully imparted to new teachers. At the moment, however, they are true exceptions. The fact that a method proves successful in their hands does not mean that it will solve important problems in education.

The Idol of the Good Student is the belief that what a good student can learn, any student can learn. Because they have superior ability or have been exposed to fortunate early environments, some students learn without being taught. It is quite possible that they learn more effectively when they are not taught. Possibly we shall someday produce more of them. At the moment, however, the fact that a method works with good students does not mean that it will work with all. It is possible that we shall progress more rapidly toward effective education by leaving the good teacher and the good student out of account altogether. They will not suffer, because they do not need our help. We may then devote ourselves to the discovery of practices which are appropriate to the remaining—what?—ninety-five per cent of teachers and students.

The Idols of the School explain some of the breathless excitement with which educational theorists return again and again to a few standard solutions. Perhaps we should regard them as merely two special cases of a more general source of error, the belief that personal experience in the classroom is the primary source of pedagogical wisdom. It is actually very difficult for teachers to profit from experience. They almost never learn about their long-term successes or failures, and their short-term effects are not easily traced to the practices from which they presumably arose. Few teachers have time to reflect on such matters, and traditional educational research has given them little help. A much more effective kind of research is now becoming possible. Teaching may be defined as an arrangement of contingencies of reinforcement under which behavior

changes. Relevant contingencies can be most successfully analyzed in studying the behavior of one student
at a time under carefully controlled conditions. Few
educators are aware of the extent to which human behavior is being examined in arrangements of this sort,
but a true technology of teaching is imminent. It is
beginning to suggest effective alternatives to the average
practices that have caused so much trouble.